O BROTHER, WHERE ART THOU?

O BROTHER,
WHERE ART THOU?

Ethan Coen
and
Joel Coen

faber and faber

First published in 2000
by Faber and Faber Limited
3 Queen Square London WC1N 3AU
Published in the United States by Faber and Faber, Inc.,
an affiliate of Farrar, Straus and Giroux LLC, New York

Photoset by Parker Typesetting Service, Leicester
Printed in England by Mackays of Chatham PLC, Chatham, Kent

Ethan Coen and Joel Coen are hereby identified as authors
of this work in accordance with Section 77 of the Copyright,
Designs and Patents Act 1988

Photographs © 2000 Touchstone Pictures and Universal Studios.
All rights reserved

A CIP record for this book
is available from the British Library

ISBN 0–571–20518–6

Special thanks to Alan Schoolcraft without
whose admirable assistance the publication of
this book would not have been possible:
Thanks are also due to Anthony Gardner and Pat Murphy.

2 4 6 8 10 9 7 5 3 1

CONTENTS

INTRODUCTION

Men it was, in the original *Odyssey*, that the Cyclops crushed and flung aside. In its modern retelling, the movie film *O Brother, Where Art Thou?*, it is a frog. The revision signals times different, changes deep.

The Cyclops' incarnation in *O Brother, Where Art Thou?* is as a one-eyed itinerant Bible salesman; he discovers a frog cached in a shoebox belonging to two amiable rustics whom he is in the process of robbing. The scene, though trite, is striking for the fact that the imprisoned frog instantly earns the viewer's identification. But – why not? Thumping blindly inside its shoebox, the panicked frog embodies the modern condition. Modern man, no longer possessing the simple confidence of the Greek sailors – indeed, bereft of mission altogether – hops fretfully about, banging his nose against limits so obscure their very nature is enigma. And too like box-bound frog, he is alone. Though he may hear muted thumps from other boxes far away, it is only desperate surmise that they betoken the strivings of creatures like himself. His impressions of the outer world are filtered and untrustworthy. All that he really knows is the darkness close by. All that is indubitable is his own anxiety.

Or perhaps there is one other certain thing. If the present inspires anxiety, the future inspires dread. Somehow in his smallness and ignorance yet he knows his fate. One day the lid shall be lifted from his shoebox and the light shall pour in – signaling not, however, that freedom has been attained. No, the fresh new air now flooding in shall prove to be the medium of a being beyond his imaginings who shall engulf him in a great godlike grip, and squish him utterly.

All dread is, at bottom, dread of being squished. If evidence for this is needed, consider our primal reaction to the sound of the frog being squished in the movie film. It is the sound, once familiar in restaurants with hard tables, of ketchup being squirted from a sputtering plastic bottle – a red cylinder whose cone-shaped cap bears, at its pierced pinnacle, congealing dribs that tell of spurts and squeezings past.

The sound of blurted ketchup at once fascinates and repels us. We used, in company with our fellows, to confront that sound. The familiar ketchup dispenser was at one time found on formica tabletops in every roadside diner and on stainless-steel counters at every ballpark concession stand; wherever men gathered and ate meat, there was its simple silhouette. The disappearance of these bottles with their intimations of mortality coincided (and no coincidence!) with the decline of the whoopee cushion, whose pseudo-gastric mutterings likewise foretold the final eruption. This, literally, is man's end: expelled air jostling squeezed-out innards as they compete for egress at every bodily opening. This, the flap and flutter of air and liquid and solid, is the sound of man's fate.

More and more, lately, we have tried to deny it. Disposable ketchup packets whose contents may be silently dispensed have everywhere replaced the communal bottle. Toothpaste tubes no longer retain the print of daily press of thumb that, accumulating and overlapping on the old wax-lined metal tube, would display its history and by extension predict its demise. No medicine cabinet now swings open to reveal tube tail upcurling like fin of sounding whale. And no more do we use garbage bags of brown pulped paper that soak up the damp and rot of their moldering contents. No; everything we handle now springs out, pops back, or is quickly swathed in plastic so that we need not witness its depletion and decay, so that we may tell ourselves that our own journey does not spend us, does not bring us closer day by day to death.

We lie. Death is ours. Art shall discover this lie. But we have changed over the millennia that separate us from the bard whose story we obsessively retell. His expeditionaries were small only in relation to giants and the gods; modern man is small, as it were, absolutely. He is frog. His world is dark. And his art, when it is honest, shows him tinged with fear.

In its day the whoopee cushion was laughed at; so do we seek to conquer our fear. No doubt the movie film *O Brother, Where Art Thou?* will likewise be laughed at, but it is the story, bleak and true, of man in our time.

Carson's Movie Abstract is a quarterly of movie synopses compiled for professionals in the humanities. The foregoing, from the Fall 2000 issue, is reprinted with permission.

O Brother, Where Art Thou?

BLACK

In black, we hear a chain-gang chant, many voices together, spaced around the unison strike of picks against rock. A title burns in:

O muse!
Sing in me, and through me tell the story
Of that man skilled in all the ways of contending,
A wanderer, harried for years on end . . .

On the sound of an impact we cut to:

A PICK

splitting a rock.

As the chant continues, wider angles show the chain-gang at work. They are black men in bleached and faded stripes, chained together, working under a brutal midday sun.

It is flat delta countryside; the straight-ruled road stretches to infinity. Mounted guards with shotguns lazily patrol the line.

The chain-gang chant is regular and, it seems, timeless.

We slowly fade out, returning to

BLACK

The last of the voices fades.

After a long beat we hear the guitar introduction to Harry McClintock's 'The Big Rock Candy Mountain'.

A WHEAT FIELD

A road cuts across the middle background. Noonday sun beats down.

We hear the distant picks and shovels of men at work and see, rising above ground level, the occasional upraised pick and spade heaving dirt. Men are digging a ditch alongside the road.

After a long beat, three men pop up in the wheat field in the middle foreground. They wear faded stripes and grey duck-billed caps. They scurry abreast toward the camera, throwing an occasional glance back at the ditch-diggers. A clanking sound accompanies their run. Oddly, the wheat between them sweeps down as they run. After a brief sprint they drop back down into the wheat.

In the background a man enters frame left, strolling along the road, wearing a khaki uniform and sunglasses, a shotgun resting against one shoulder. He glances idly down into the ditch and strolls on out of frame right.

The three men rise back up from the wheat and, clanking, resume their sprint.

THREE PAIRS OF EYES

They are topped by three cap bills, and peer out from behind a blind of greenery. We hear distant whistling.

The men are looking at a weathered barn. A young boy, whistling, is heading down the road that leads away from the barn, jiggling the traces of the old plough horse that leads him. He turns a corner and is gone.

BARNYARD

The three clanking men (we can now see their leg irons) are awkwardly chasing a chicken around the yard. The squawking yardbird doesn't need to move much to elude the three bunched men.

COUNTRY LANE

It curves in a gentle S into the background. It is sun-dappled, pretty.

We hear clanking footsteps approaching at a trot.

The three men enter in the foreground and trot on down the lane. The leftmost has a flapping chicken tucked under one arm.

AFTERNOON CAMPFIRE

The three men sit in a side-by-side arc around a dying fire, one of them contentedly picking his teeth with a small chicken bone, another wiping

4

grease off his chin with a sleeve, the third idly poking at the fire with a spit.

Each of them, still bound by chains, clinks as he moves.

One of them abruptly cocks his head, listening.

The others notice his attitude and also freeze, listening.

We hear the distant baying of hounds.

ROLLING HILLS

From high on a ridge we see the three chained men running toward us.

In addition to their clanks we hear a distant chugging sound.

TRACKING

Laterally with the clanking, running feet.

The chugging sound is very loud.

RUNNING

Next to a freight train. A boxcar door is open.

INSIDE THE BOXCAR

The lead convict hooks an elbow in and starts hauling himself up, his two clanking friends keeping pace outside.

Six hobos sit in the boxcar, lounging against sacks of O'Daniel's Flour. They impassively watch the convict clamber in as his two confederates run to keep up.

The convict hauls himself to his feet. In spite of his stubble he has carefully tended hair and a pencil mustache. He is Everett.

As he dusts himself off:

EVERETT

Say, uh, any a you boys smithies?

The hobos stare.

Everett gives an ingratiating smile as, behind him, the second convict starts to haul himself into the boxcar, the third convict still keeping pace outside.

Or, if not smithies *per se*, were you otherwise trained in the metallurgic arts before straitened circumstances forced you into a life of aimless wanderin'?

The convict running outside the boxcar door stumbles and disappears and the middle convict is yanked out immediately after. Everett, just finishing his speech, flips forward in turn, smashes his chin onto the floor and is sucked out the open doorway, his clawing fingernails leaving parallel grooves on the boxcar floorboards.

The hobos impassively watch.

OUTSIDE

The three men tumble, clanking, down the track embankment.

Squush – they come to rest in swampland at the bottom.

They shake their heads clear, then rise to their feet in the muck and watch the train recede.

Its fading clatter leaves the baying of hounds.

> EVERETT
> Jesus – can't I count on you people?

The second con is Delmar.

> DELMAR
> Sorry, Everett.

Everett looks desperately about.

> EVERETT
> All right – if we take off through that bayou –

The third con, Pete, bald but also with beard stubble, angrily cuts in:

> PETE
> Wait a minute! Who elected *you* leader a this outfit?

EVERETT.

Well, Pete, I just figured it should be the one with capacity for abstract thought. But if that ain't the consensus view, hell, let's put her to a vote!

PETE

Suits me! I'm votin' for yours truly!

EVERETT

Well *I'm* votin' for yours truly *too*!

Both men look interrogatively to Delmar.

He looks from Pete to Everett, and nods agreeably.

DELMAR

Okay – I'm with you fellas.

Everett makes a sudden hushing gesture and all listen.

The baying of hounds is louder now, but through it we hear a distant scrape of metal against metal, like the workings of a rusty pump. The men turn in unison to look up the track.

A small, distant form is moving slowly up the track toward them.

As it draws closer it resolves into a human-propelled flatcar. An ancient black man rhythmically pumps its long seesaw handle.

The three convicts look out at the swampland which begins to show movement, the bowing grass trampled by men and dogs.

The flatcar draws even and slows.

EVERETT

Mind if we join you, ol' timer?

OLD MAN

Join me, my sons.

The three men clamber aboard and the old man resumes pumping.

The three men exchange glances; Delmar waves a clanking hand before the old man's milky eyes. No reaction.

DELMAR

You work for the railroad, grandpa?

OLD MAN

I work for no man.

PETE

Got a name, do ya?

OLD MAN

I have no name.

EVERETT

Well, that right there may be why you've had difficulty finding gainful employment. Ya see, in the mart of competitive commerce, the –

OLD MAN

You seek a great fortune, you three who are now in chains
. . .

The men fall silent.

. . . And you will find a fortune – though it will not be the fortune you seek . . .

8

The three convicts, faces upturned, listen raptly to the blind prophet.

> . . . But first, first you must travel – a long and difficult road –
> a road fraught with peril, uh-huh, and pregnant with
> adventure. You shall see things wonderful to tell. You shall
> see a cow on the roof of a cottonhouse, uh-huh, and oh, so
> many startlements . . .

*The cloudy eyes of the old man stare sightlessly down the track as the
seesaw handle rises and falls through frame.*

> . . . I cannot say how long this road shall be. But fear not the
> obstacles in your path, for Fate has vouchsafed your reward.
> And though the road may wind, and yea, your hearts grow
> weary, still shall ye foller the way, even unto your salvation.

The old man pumps – reek-a reek-a reek-a – as all contemplate his words.

Loud and sudden:

> – Izzat clear?!

The men start, then mumble polite acknowledgment.

*The railroad tracks wind to the setting sun. Reek-a reek-a reek-a reek-a
– the flatcar rolls, in wide shot, toward the golden horizon.*

FADE OUT

DAY

A hot dusty road leading up to a lone farmhouse.

The three men walk, clanking and abreast.

DELMAR

How'd he know about the treasure?

EVERETT

Don't know, Delmar – though the blind are reputed to
possess sensitivities compensatin' for their lack of sight, even
to the point of developing para-normal psychic powers. Now
clearly, seein' the future would fall neatly into that ka-taggery.
It's not so surprising, then, if an organism deprived of earthly
vision –

He said we wouldn't get it! He said we wouldn't get the
treasure we seek!

Everett grows testy:

EVERETT

Well what does he know – he's a ignorant old man! Jesus,
Pete, I'm telling you I buried it myself, and if your cousin still
runs this-here horse farm and has a forge and some shoein'
impedimenta to restore our liberty of movement –

Bang! A rifle shot kicks up dust in front of the men.

CHILD'S VOICE

Hold it rah chair!

*The front of the farm house shows only a harshly shaded front porch and
a dark screen door.*

*The screen door swings open and a child emerges on to the porch and
steps down into the sunlight, holding a gun almost bigger than he is. The
grimy-faced boy, about eight years old, wears tattered overalls.*

You men from the bank?

PETE

You Wash's boy?

CHILD

Yassir! And Daddy tolt me I'm to shoot whosoever from the
bank!

He pokes his rifle at the three men, who raise their hands.

DELMAR

Well, we ain't from no bank, young feller.

CHILD

Yassir! I'm also suppose to shoot folks servin' papers!

DELMAR

Well we ain't got no papers.

CHILD

Yassir! I nicked the census man!

IO

DELMAR

There's a good boy. Is your daddy about?

THE BACK OF THE HOUSE

Wash Hogwallop, a sour-looking bald man, sits near a rusted bathtub in a yard littered with ancient car parts and farm implements overgrown with weeds. He is whittling artlessly at a stick.

He glances up as the three convicts clank around the corner, then returns to his whittling.

WASH

'Lo, Pete. Hooor yer friends?

EVERETT

Pleased to make your acquaintance, Mister Hogwallop. M'name's Ulysses Everett McGill.

DELMAR

'N I'm Delmar O'Donnell.

PETE

How ya been, Wash? Been what, twelve, thirteen year'n?

Still looking sourly at his whittling:

WASH

You've grown chatty.

He tosses the stick aside and sighs.

I expect you'll want them chains knocked off.

THE HOGWALLOP KITCHEN

The four men and little boy sit around the kitchen table eating stew. A Sears Roebuck catalogue on the boy's chair brings him to table height. The cons are now rid of their chains and are dressed in ill-fitting farmer's wear.

WASH

They foreclosed on Cousin Vester. He hanged himself a year come May.

PETE

And Uncle Ratliff?

WASH

The anthrax took most of his cows. The rest don't milk, and he lost a boy to mumps.

PETE

Where's Cora, Cousin Wash?

Wash glances at the little boy.

WASH

Couldn't say. Mrs Hogwallop up and R–U–N–N–O–F–T.

EVERETT

Mm. Must've been lookin' for answers.

WASH

Possibly. Good riddance, far as I'm concerned . . .

The three men slurp their stew.

I do miss her cookin' though.

DELMAR

This stew's awful good.

WASH

Think so?

He sniffs dubiously at his spoon.

I slaughtered this horse last Tuesday; 'm afraid she's startin' to turn.

LIVING ROOM

Later. The four men sit about listening to a big box radio. Wash is whittling once again; Everett dips his comb into a pomade jar and carefully works on his hair; Pete is digging around with a toothpick; Delmar dreamily waves one hand in time to the music.

The music ends.

Well, that's the last number for tonight's 'Pass the Biscuits Pappy O'Daniel Flour Hour'. This is Pappy O'Daniel, hopin' you folks been enjoyin' that good old-timey music, and remember, when you're fixin' to fry up some flapjacks or bake a mess a biscuits, use cool clear water and good pure Pappy O'Daniel flour for that 'Pass the Biscuits, Pappy' flavor. So tune in next week folks, and till then whyncha turn to your better half and sing along with Pappy: 'You are my sunshine, my only sunshine . . .'

Everett clears his throat.

EVERETT
Well, guess I'll be turning in . . .

He screws the lid back on the pomade.

Say, Cousin Wash, I guess it'd be the acme of foolishness to enquire if you had a hairnet.

WASH
Got a bunch in yon byurra. Mrs Hogwallop's, matter of fact. Hepyaseff; I won't be needin' 'em.

THE THREE MEN

Sleeping in a hayloft. Everett wears a hairnet over his painstakingly arranged hair.

Pete snores on the inhale. Delmar whistles on the exhale.

A spotlight plays over the hayloft ceiling and a voice booms:

BULLHORN VOICE
All right boys, itsy authorities.

The three men rouse themselves.

We gotcha surrounded. Just come on out grabbin' air!

Everett shrugs into his suspenders and peeks down into the barnyard.

EVERETT
Damn! We're in a tight spot!

From high we see a foreshortened lawman holding a bullhorn surrounded by armed deputies.

Next to the man with the bullhorn, a tin-starred sheriff watches impassively through mirrored sunglasses, a bloodhound drooling at his side.

MAN WITH BULLHORN
And don't try nothin' fancy – your sitchy-ation is purt nigh hopeless.

DELMAR
What inna Sam Hill . . . ?

EVERETT
Pete's cousin turned us in for the bounty!

PETE
The hell you say. Wash is kin!

An unamplified voice echoes up from the yard:

VOICE
Sorry Pete! I know we're kin! But they got this Depression on, and I gotta do fer me and mine!

Pete screams down from the hayport:

PETE
I'M GONNA KILL YOU, JUDAS ISCARIOT HOGWALLOP! YOU MIS'ABLE HOSS-EATIN' SONOFABITCH! YOU –

RAT-A-TAT-A-TAT – Everett pulls Pete down as a tommy gun spits lead into the hayloft.

EVERETT
Damn! We're in a tight spot!

Pete is enraged:

PETE
Damn his eyes! Pa always said never trust a Hogwallop – COME'N GET US, COPPERS!

BULLHORN VOICE

So be it! You boys're leavin' us no choice but to smoke you out.

EVERETT

Oh no! Lord have mercy . . .

Men approach the barn with torches.

DELMAR

What do we do now, Everett?

EVERETT

Fire! I hate fire!

PETE

YOU LOUSY TIN-WEARIN' MOTHERLESS
BARNBURNIN' COCKAROACHES –

Everett cuts in, his voice breaking:

EVERETT

NOW HOLD ON, BOYS – AINTCHA EVER HEARD
OF A NEGOTIATION? MAYBE WE CAN TALK
THIS THING OUT!

DELMAR

Yeah, let's negotiate 'em, Everett.

The hayloft is filling with smoke. Flames lick downstairs.

PETE

YOU LOUSY YELLA-BELLIED LOW-DOWN
SKUNKS –

EVERETT

Now hold on, Pete, we gotta speak with one voice here –
CAREFUL WITH THAT FIRE NOW, BOYS!

Pete grabs a flaming faggot and hurls it down at the deputized congregation.

It lands harmlessly in some scattered straw.

BULLHORN VOICE

You choose it, boys – the prison farm or the pearly gates!

The straw curls, lights, and the fire scuttles over to a parked Black Maria.

With a loud airy WHOOOF! the undercarriage of the police van pops into flame.

The man with the bullhorn sees it.

> **MAN WITH BULLHORN**
> Holy Saint Christopher – OUTA THAT VEHICLE, CHAMP, SHE'S LICKIN' FAR!

Tommy guns are stored in the back of the van. The drum of one starts spinning.

Flames lick up the outside of the van as – chinka-chinka-chinka – bullet holes walk across the body.

> Take cover, boys, THAT AIN'T POPCORN!

Yelling men scurry away.

The vehicle rocks and chatters under the force of the many tommy guns now firing inside. Tires pop, hiss and settle; doors pop open; glass shatters.

Who's that?

An oncoming car is bouncing crazily across the yard, horn blaring. Deputies leap out of its path.

The car shoots past the chattering van which still bucks and bounces on its shocks, its interior strobing and flashing as if with trapped lightning.

The speeding car heads directly for the flaming barn door and crashes through in a shower of sparks.

The car brakes inside the barn and the driver's door flies open. The little Hogwallop boy yells over the roar of the flames:

BOY
Come on, boys! I'm gonna R–U–N–N–O–F–T!

Pete, Everett and Delmar pile in.

DELMAR
You should be in bed, little fella.

The doors slam shut and the boy grinds into gear. He has wood blocks strapped to his feet so that he can reach accelerator, brake and clutch. He sits on a Sears Roebuck catalogue to give him a view over the dash.

BOY
You ain't the boss a me!

The car speeds for the far wall, sheeted in flame, and bursts through.

COUNTRY ROAD DAY

The little Hogwallop boy walks away in long shot down the middle of the empty road. His walk is unsteady, the wood blocks still strapped to his feet.

He turns to face us and hollers:

BOY
You candy-butted car-thievin' so's 'n so's! I curse yer names!

Pete enters in the foreground and throws a dirt clod at the boy. It lands shy as Pete yells:

Go back home'n mind yer pa!

We pan Pete over to the shoulder where the car is stopped, its hood propped open. Everett and Delmar are looking at the engine.

What's the damn problem?

DRYGOODS STORE

The proprietor is a bespectacled middle-aged man wearing sleeve garters and a visor. Behind him are stacked, among other necessaries, sacks of O'Daniel Flour. He pushes a small tin across the counter.

PROPRIETOR
I can get the part from Bristol; it'll take two weeks. Here's your pomade.

Everett is stunned:

EVERETT
Two weeks! That don't do me no good!

PROPRIETOR
Nearest Ford auto man's Bristol.

Everett picks up the tin.

EVERETT
Hold on there – I don't want this pomade, I want Dapper Dan.

PROPRIETOR
I don't carry Dapper Dan. I carry Fop.

EVERETT
No! I don't want Fop! Goddamnit – I use Dapper Dan!

PROPRIETOR
Watch your language, young fellow, this is a public market. Now, if you want Dapper Dan I can order it for you, have it in a couple of weeks.

EVERETT
Well, ain't this place a geographical oddity – two weeks from everywhere! Forget it! Just the dozen hairnets!

PETE AND DELMAR

On a wooded hillside. They sit at a twig fire, roasting a small creature on a spit.

EVERETT
(*off*)
It didn't *look* like a one-horse town . . .

He stalks into frame and plops disgustedly down by the fire.

. . . but *try* getting a decent hair jelly.

DELMAR
Gopher, Everett?

EVERETT
And no transmission belt for two weeks neither.

PETE
Huh?! They dam that river on the 21st. Today's the 17th!

EVERETT
Don't I know it.

PETE
We got but four days to get to that treasure! After that, it'll be at the bottom of a lake!

He grimly shakes his head.

We ain't gonna make it walkin'.

DELMAR
Gopher, Everett?

Everett has taken out a can of near-empty Dapper Dan. He scrapes the last of it onto his comb and starts combing his hair.

We hear distant singing – one lone tenor voice.

EVERETT
Well you're right there, but the ol' tactician's already got a plan –

Everett fishes a gold watch from his pocket and tosses it to Pete.

– for the transportation, that is; I don't know how I'm gonna
keep my coiffure in order.

Pete looks at the watch, puzzled.

> PETE
>
> How's this a plan? How're we gonna get a car?

> EVERETT
>
> Sell that. I figured it could only have painful associations for
> Wash.

Pete pops the front and reads the inscription:

> PETE
>
> To Washington Bartholomew Hogwallop. From his loving
> Cora. Ay-More Fie-dellis.

> EVERETT
>
> It was in his bureau.

He screws the lid back on the pomade.

> I reckon it'll fetch us enough cash for a good used auto-
> voiture and maybe a little left over besides.

The singing is growing louder.

Delmar whistles appreciatively.

> DELMAR
>
> You got light fingers, Everett. Gopher?

> PETE
>
> You mis'able little sneak thief . . .

He lurches threateningly to his feet.

> You stole from my kin!

Everett scrambles up.

> EVERETT
>
> – Who was fixing to betray us!

> PETE
>
> You didn't know that at the time!

EVERETT

So I borrowed it till I *did* know!

PETE

That don't make no sense!

EVERETT

Pete, it's a fool looks for logic in the chambers of the human heart. What the hell's that singing?

We can make out the words now, sung by the lone tenor.

VOICE

Oh Brothers, let's go down,
Come on down,
Don't you wanna go down . . .

People in white robes are drifting down the hill, through the woods behind the campsite. They join in with the lead voice:

VOICES

Oh Brothers, let's go down,
Down to the river to pray . . .

Delmar gazes wonderingly at the white-robed figures as he answers Everett:

DELMAR

Appears to be . . . some kinda . . . con-gur-gation. Care for some gopher?

Everett too watches the white-robed people following in the wake of the tenor. He answers absently:

EVERETT

No, thank you Delmar – a third of a gopher would only rouse my appetite without beddin' her back down.

There are more and more white robes drifting through the woods, all of them strangely oblivious to the three men.

DELMAR

You can have the whole thing – me'n Pete already had one . . .

There is an endless stream now, drifting through the foreground, the background, the campsite itself.

VOICES
Oh, Sisters, let's go down,
Come on down,
Don't you want to go down . . .

DELMAR
We ran acrost a gopher village . . .

The drifting worshipers wear beatific expressions. One only, a middle-aged woman, notices the three convicts around whom the rest of the flock blindly drifts. She calls to them:

WOMAN
Come with us, brothers! Join us and be saved!

THE RIVER

White robes stream down the hill, out of the woods, and down the riverbank. The voices swell in a great chorus:

VOICES
We went down to the river one day,

Studying about that good old way,
And who shall wear that robe and crown,
Oh Lord, show us the way . . .

We are booming down to reveal a minister in the foreground. He stands belly-deep in the river, easing a white-robed man back-down into the water. Behind him a line of robed singers lengthens steadily as people stream out of the woods.

Pete, Delmar and Everett emerge from the woods and gaze down at the river. White-robed people continue to drift past them.

> EVERETT
I guess hard times flush the chumps. Everybody's lookin' for answers, and there's always –

Delmar wades out into the stream, cutting in line.

Where the hell's he goin'?

Delmar has reached the minister and holds his nose as the minister incantates over him and lowers him into the river.

> PETE
Well, I'll be a sonofabitch. Delmar's been saved!

EVERETT

Pete, don't be ignorant –

Delmar is slogging back through the water.

DELMAR

Well that's it boys, I been redeemed! The preacher warshed away all my sins and transgressions. It's the straight-and-narrow from here on out and heaven everlasting's my reward!

EVERETT

Delmar what the hell are you talking about? – We got bigger fish to fry –

DELMAR

Preacher said my sins are warshed away, including that Piggly Wiggly I knocked over in Yazoo!

EVERETT

I thought you said you were innocent a those charges.

DELMAR

Well I was lyin' – and I'm proud to say that that sin's been warshed away too! Neither God nor man's got nothin' on me now! Come on in, boys, the water's fine!

LATER

The smoldering twig fire. A bloodhound on a leash circles into frame, its tail fiercely wagging.

We follow it as, nose to the ground and straining against its leash, it waddles over to an empty tin of Dapper Dan pomade.

A VOICE

All right, boys! We got the scent!

A CAR

Everett drives, shaking his head with a forebearing smile. Pete, sitting next to him, and Delmar, in back, are both dripping wet.

Pete is sullen:

PETE

The preacher said it absolved us.

EVERETT

For him, not for the law! I'm surprised at you, Pete. Hell, I gave you credit for more brains than Delmar.

DELMAR

But there were witnesses, *saw* us redeemed!

EVERETT

That's not the issue, Delmar. Even if it did put you square with the Lord, the State of Mississippi is more hardnosed.

DELMAR

You should a joined us, Everett. It couldn't a hurt none.

PETE

Hell, at least it woulda washed away the stink of that pomade.

EVERETT

Join you two ignorant fools in a ridiculous superstition? Thank you anyway. And I *like* the smell of my hair treatment – the pleasing odor is half the point.

He shakes his head and laughs.

Baptism. You two are just dumber'n a bag of hammers. Well, I guess you're my cross to bear –

DELMAR
Pull over, Everett – let's give that colored boy a lift.

A thirtyish black man in worn go-to-meetin' clothes stands on the shoulder, waggling his thumb at the passing car. He grabs his battered guitar case as the car pulls over and trots up to the open window.

HITCHHIKER
You folks goin' through Tishamingo?

Delmar pushes open the back door.

DELMAR
Sure, hop in.

Everett looks at the man in the rearview mirror as he pulls out.

EVERETT
How ya doin', boy? Name's Everett, and these two soggy sonsabitches are Pete and Delmar. Keep your fingers away from Pete's mouth – he ain't had nothin' to eat for the last thirteen years but prison food, gopher, and a little greasy horse.

HITCHHIKER
Thank you fuh the lif', suh. M'names Tommy. Tommy Johnson.

Delmar is genuinely friendly:

DELMAR
How ya doin', Tommy. I haven't seen a house in miles. What're you doin' out in the middle of nowhere?

Tommy is matter-of-fact:

TOMMY
I had to be at that crossroads las' midnight to sell mah soul to the devil.

EVERETT
Well ain't it a small world, spiritually speakin'! Pete and

Delmar just been baptized and saved! I guess I'm the only one here who remains unaffiliated!

DELMAR
This ain't no laughin' matter, Everett.

EVERETT
What'd the devil give you for your soul, Tommy?

TOMMY
He taught me to play this guitar real good.

Delmar is horrified:

DELMAR
Oh, son! For that you traded your everlastin' soul?!

Tommy shrugs.

TOMMY
I wudden usin' it.

PETE
I always wondered – what's the devil look like?

EVERETT
Well, of course there's all manner of lesser imps'n demons, Pete, but the Great Satan hisself is red and scaly with a bifurcated tail and carries a hayfork.

TOMMY
Oh no! No suh! He's white – white as you folks, with mirrors for eyes an' a big hollow voice an' allus travels with a mean old hound.

PETE
And he told you to go to Tishamingo?

TOMMY
No suh, that was mah idea. I heard they's a man there pays folks money to sing into a can. They say he pays extra effen you play real good.

Everett's eyes narrow as he studies the man in the rearview.

EVERETT
How much does he pay?

TISHAMINGO

The car is pulling into the parking lot of a single-story cement-block building with a hundred-foot antenna and a handpainted sign:

WEZY
Listening Ain't Never Been
So Easy Nor
So Fine

As the men get out of the car, Everett snaps his suspenders.

EVERETT
All right boys, just follow my lead.

INSIDE

Everett strides up to a portly middle-aged man who wears dark glasses and holds a white cane.

EVERETT
Who's the honcho around here?

MAN
I am. Hur you?

EVERETT
Well sir, my name is Jordan Rivers and these here are The Soggy Bottom Boys outta Cottonelia Mississippi – Songs of Salvation to Salve the Soul. We hear you pay good money to sing into a can.

MAN
Well that all depends. You boys do Negro songs?

Everett grimaces, thinking.

EVERETT
Sir, we *are* Negroes. All except our a-cump – uh, company – accompluh – uh, the fella that plays the gui-tar.

MAN

Well, I don't record Negro songs. I'm lookin' for some ol'-
timey material. Why, people just can't get enough of it since
we started broadcastin' the 'Pappy O'Daniel Flour Hour', so
thanks for stoppin' by, but –

EVERETT

Sir, the Soggy Bottom Boys been *steeped* in ol'-timey material.
Heck, you're silly with it, aintcha boys?

PETE

That's right!

DELMAR

That's right! We ain't really Negroes!

PETE

All except fer our a-cump-uh-nust!

THE STUDIO

*The three singing convicts form a semi-circle behind Tommy, who plays
his guitar into a can microphone. They are performing a hot and
harmonized version of 'Man of Constant Sorrow'.*

When they finish Everett whoops and slaps Tommy on the back.

EVERETT

Hot damn, boy, I almost believe you *did* sell your soul to the
devil!

MAN

Boys, that was some mighty fine pickin' and a-singin'. You
just sign these papers and I'll give you ten dollars apiece.

EVERETT

Okay sir, but Mert and Aloysius'll have to scratch Xes – only
four of us can write.

THE LOT

*A caravan of two oversize cars is pulling into the lot just as Tommy and
the three convicts burst out of the station door, whooping it up.*

A sixty-year-old man in enormous seersucker pants held up by suspenders and the outward pressure of a blooming belly is getting out of the first car. His face is familiar from countless sacks of Pass the Biscuits Pappy O'Daniel Flour.

Delmar waves a fistful of money at him.

DELMAR
Hey mister! I don't mean to be tellin' tales out a school, but there's a man in there hands out ten dollars to anyone sings into his can!

PAPPY
I'm not here to make a record, ya dumb cracker, they broadcast me out on the radio.

A big shambling man of about thirty has followed him out of the car. He has the sloping shoulders, the pasty skin, and the aimlessly bobbing head of an intellectual flyweight.

JUNIOR
That's Governor Menelaus 'Pass the Biscuits, Pappy' O'Daniel, and he'd sure 'preciate it if you ate his farina and voted him a second term.

Two other members of the retinue, older men whose girth rivals the governor's, are Eckard and Spivey.

ECKARD

Finest governor we've ever had in M'sippi.

SPIVEY

In any state.

ECKARD

Oh Lord yes, any parish'r precinct; I was makin' the larger point.

As Pappy brushes by them, Junior wheedles:

JUNIOR

Aintcha gonna press the flesh, Pappy, do a little politickin'?

Pappy slaps at the young man with his hat.

PAPPY

I'll press *your* flesh, you dimwitted sonofabitch – you don't tell your pappy how to cawt the elect' rate!

Pappy waves his hat at the radio building as singers in faux *hillbilly outfits with various musical instrument cases get out of the second car.*

We ain't one-at-a-timin' here, we *mass* communicatin'!

ECKARD

Oh, yes, assa parful new force.

SPIVEY

Mm-mm.

The men head for the station, with Junior lagging.

PAPPY

Shake a leg, Junior! Thank God your mama died givin' birth
– if she'd a seen ya she'd a died of shame . . .

A CAMPFIRE

It is night.

*Tommy sits in the background, playing and singing a slow blues. The
three convicts, holding coffee cups, gaze into the fire.*

Over the dreamy song:

DELMAR

Why don't we bed down out here tonight?

PETE

Yeah, it stinks in that ol' barn.

EVERETT

Suits me . . .

He stretches out.

Pretty soon it'll be nothin' but feather beds'n silk sheets.

Pete swishes his coffee as he stares into the blaze.

PETE

A million dollars.

EVERETT

Million point *two*.

DELMAR

Five . . . hunnert . . . thousand . . . each.

EVERETT

Four hundred, Delmar.

DELMAR

Izzat right?

EVERETT

What're you gonna do with your share of the treasure, Pete?

PETE

Go out west somewhere, open a fine restaurant. I'm gonna be the maider dee. Greet all the swells, go to work ever' day in a bowtie and tuxedo, an' the staff'll all say Yassir and Nawsir and In a Jiffy Pete . . .

He gives his coffee a thoughtful swish and murmurs:

An' all my meals for free . . .

EVERETT

What about you, Delmar? What're you gonna do with your share a that dough?

DELMAR

Visit those foreclosin' sonofaguns down at the Indianola Savings and Loan and slap that cash down on the barrelhead and buy back the family farm. Hell, you ain't no kind of man if you ain't got land.

PETE

What about you, Everett? What'd you have in mind when you stoled it in the first place?

EVERETT

Me? Oh, I didn't have no plan. Still don't, really.

PETE

Well that hardly sounds like you . . .

A distant voice:

VOICE

All right, boys, itsy authorities!

The three men tense up. Tommy stops singing.

33

Your sitchy-ation is purt nigh hopeless!

Pete shovels dirt onto the fire as Delmar and Everett scramble to peek over a low ridge.

Their point-of-view shows a lone barn with their car parked to one side. Various police vehicles have pulled up facing the barn, and armed men, their backs to us, train guns on it, some taking cover on the near side of their parked cars.

EVERETT
Damn! They found our car!

The man with the bullhorn continues, directing his comments at the distant barn:

MAN
We ain't got the time – and nary inclination – to gentle you boys no further!

The three convicts notice the sheriff who once again stands impassively next to the man with the bullhorn, holding a leash against which a bloodhound strains.

It's either the penal farm or the fires of damnation – makes no nevermind to me!

The sheriff makes a signal to a man holding a torch, who skitters up to the barn and lights it.

DELMAR
Damn! We gotta skedaddle!

EVERETT
I left my pomade in that car! Maybe I can creep up!

DELMAR
Don't be a fool, Everett, we gotta R–U–N–N–O–F–T, but pronto!

EVERETT
Where's Tommy?

PETE
Already lit out, scared out of his wits. Let's go!

DAYTIME ROAD

The three men shuffle down the dusty road.

> PETE
>
> The hell it *ain't* square one! Ain't no one gonna pick up three filthy unshaved hitchhikers, and one of 'em a know-it-all that can't keep his trap shut!

> EVERETT
>
> Pete, the personal rancor reflected in that remark I don't intend to dignify with comment, but I *would* like to address your general attitude of hopeless negativism. Consider the lilies a the goddamn field, or – hell! – take a look at Delmar here as your paradigm a hope.

> DELMAR
>
> Yeah, look at me.

> EVERETT
>
> Now you may call it an unreasoning optimism. You may call it obtuse. But the plain fact is we still have . . . close to . . . close to . . .

He loses his drift as all three men turn, reacting to the sound of an approaching speeding car.

. . . close to . . . three days . . . before they dam that river . . .

The car comes into view cornering on two wheels. It crashes back onto all four and, as it speeds along, dollar bills snap and flutter out its windows. The car roars up to the three men as Delmar waggles a hopeful thumb. It screeches to a halt.

The driver, a young man in a sharp suit with a round, babylike face, leans over to call through the passenger window:

> **DRIVER**
> Is this the road to Itta Bena?

> **PETE**
> Uh . . . Itta Bena . . .

Delmar plucks a fluttering dollar bill out of the air and looks at it wonderingly. He holds it stretched between two hands, brings the two sides together, then gives it an appraising pop.

> **EVERETT**
> Itta Bena, now, uh, that would be . . .

> **PETE**
> Isn't it, uh . . .

Like a child gazing at soap bubbles, Delmar looks around at the wafting currency, and yanks another fluttering bill out of the air.

EVERETT

I'm thinkin' it's uh, you could take this road to, uh . . .

There is the sound of a distant siren.

The driver, still patiently leaning over to hear out the two brainwrackers, shoots a quick look in his rearview mirror.

PETE

. . . Nah, that ain't right . . . I'm thinkin' of . . .

EVERETT

. . . I believe, unless I'm very much mistaken – see, we've been away for several years, uh . . .

The driver pushes open the passenger door.

DRIVER

Hop on in while you give it a think.

The three men climb in and the car squeals out.

INT. CAR

The driver shoots a glance up to the rearview mirror as the sirens grow louder, then gropes inside his coat.

MAN

Any a you boys know your way around a Walther PPK?

DELMAR

Well now, that's where we cain't help ya. I don't believe it's in Mississippi.

The man stops withdrawing the gun and appraises his passengers. Delmar reacts to the paper currency fluttering inside the car:

Friend, some of your folding money has come unstowed.

DRIVER

Just stuff it down that sack there. You boys aren't badmen, I take it?

37

DELMAR

Well, funny you should ask – I *was* bad, till yesterday, but me'n Pete here been saved. My name's Delmar, and that there's Everett.

DRIVER

George Nelson. It's a pleasure.

He opens his door and steps onto the running board, giving Everett a casual:

Grab the tiller, will ya buddy?

Everett slides over, startled. George Nelson, now fully outside and facing the pursuit vehicles, has one hand clamped on the car roof and waves to Delmar with the other.

Hand up that Thompson, Jack.

Delmar gropes in the footwell.

DELMAR

Say, what line of work are you in, George?

EXT. CAR

Nelson sends a spray of bullets back at the pursuit car.

NELSON

COME AND GET ME, COPPERS! YOU FLATFOOTED LAMEBRAINED SOFT-ASSED SONOFABITCHES! NO ONE CAN CATCH ME! I'M GEORGE NELSON! I'M BIGGER THAN ANY JOHN LAW EVER LIVED! HA-HA-HA-HA-HA! I'M TEN-AND-A-HALF FEET TALL AND AIN'T YET FULLY GROWED!

Nelson fires wildly as the pursuit cars gain on him, returning fire. He suddenly notices a herd of cattle grazing at the roadside and murmurs:

. . . COWS . . .

He swings the tommy gun over with a whoop.

I hate cows worse than coppers!

He lets loose a spray. One of the cows drops and the rest stampede toward the road.

DELMAR

Aww, George, not the livestock.

Energized, Nelson resumes bellowing:

NELSON

HA-HA! COME ON YOU MISERABLE SALARIED SONSABITCHES! COME AND GET ME!

In bovine ignorance of the conventions of high-speed police pursuit, some of the cows have wandered up onto the road. The lead police car broadsides one. George Nelson, cackling wildly, fires into the air as his car recedes.

SMALL TOWN

The car is speeding into town, dodging and weaving through light traffic as George fires into the air – perhaps a means of clearing a path, perhaps an expression of high spirits.

The car screeches to a halt and George hops out, and the three convicts emerge to follow him.

NELSON

COME ON BOYS! WE'RE GOIN' FOR THE RECORD – THREE BANKS IN TWO HOURS!

Jowls shaking in a full run, George Nelson bursts through the door of the bank, followed by the three men.

He fires into the ceiling and leaps up onto a table.

OKAY FOLKS! HOLD THE APPLAUSE AND DROP YER DRAWERS – I'M GEORGE NELSON AND I'M HERE TO SACK THE CITY A ITTA BENA!

He leaps down, fires into the air again, and sweeps a young woman standing on line into a full V-J dip, kissing her on the lips.

Delmar nudges Everett.

39

DELMAR

He's a live wire though, ain't he?

NELSON

Thanky dear! All the money in the bag, and you can tell your grandkids you were done by the best! I'M GEORGE NELSON AND I'M FEELIN' TEN FEET TALL!

He winks at the three men who obediently wait.

It's a kick and a quarter, ain't it boys?

Distant sirens again.

EVERETT

Pardon me, George, but have you got a plan for gettin' outa here?

NELSON

Sure boys, here's m'plan!

He whips open his suitcoat to reveal a half-dozen sticks of dynamite.

They ain't never seen ordnance like this! WELL, THANK YOU, FOLKS, AND REMEMBER: JESUS SAVES, BUT GEORGE NELSON WITHDRAWS! HA-HA-HA-HA-HA! GO FETCH THE AUTO-VOITURE, PETE!

He sends a burst into the ceiling, and heads for the door as customers murmur.

VOICE

. . . it's Babyface Nelson . . .

George whirls.

NELSON

WHO SAID THAT?!

The customers stare mutely back.

WHAT IGNORANT LOWDOWN SLANDERIZING SONOFABITCH SAID THAT?! MY NAME IS *GEORGE* NELSON, GET ME?!

The customers shuffle their feet and glance uncomfortably about. Delmar lays a hand on George's shoulder and tries to steer him toward the door.

DELMAR
They didn't mean anything by it, George.

NELSON
GEORGE NELSON! NOT BABYFACE! YOU REMEMBER AND YOU TELL YOUR FRIENDS! I'M GEORGE NELSON, BORN TO RAISE HELL!

OUTSIDE THE BANK

The siren grows louder as the four men emerge.

EVERETT
You gotta be a little tolerant, George; all these poor folk know is the legend. Hell, they can't be expected to appreciate the complex individual underneath –

NELSON
Aww, I'm all right.

He shrugs off Everett's hand and lights the fuse on a stick of dynamite.

This'll put me right back on top!

The car squeals up and, as sirens approach once again, the three men pile in.

OR-VOIR, ITTA BENA! GEORGE NELSON THANKS YOU FOR YOUR SUPPORT!

As the car peels out – KA-BOOM! – the dynamite blows a crater in the street behind.

CAMPFIRE

It is night.

George Nelson, now strangely quiet, holds a coffee cup and stares gloomily into the fire.

After a long beat, Delmar, also staring into the fire, slaps one knee and ejaculates:

DELMAR

Damn but that was some fun though, won it George?!

George responds, barely audible and without brightening:

GEORGE

. . . yeah . . .

Everett and Pete exchange significant looks. Delmar, however, is less sensitive to the Babyface's mood.

DELMAR

Almost makes me wish I hadn't been saved! Jackin' up banks – I can see how a fella could derive a lot a pleasure and satisfaction out of it!

GEORGE

. . . it's okay . . .

DELMAR

Whoa doggies!

At length George swishes the coffee around his cup, shrugs, tosses the coffee and rises.

GEORGE
. . . Well, I'm takin' off.

He digs into a pocket and tosses his car keys to a dumbfounded Delmar.

You boys can have the automobile.

Glassy-eyed, he continues to dig in his pockets and lets his money fall to the ground.

'N might as well take my share a the riches.

DELMAR
What the – where you goin', George?

George has turned woodenly and walks away, leaving the campfire's flickering circle of light.

GEORGE
. . . I dunno . . . who cares . . .

Delmar stares at Everett, who looks appraisingly at George's retreating back. Pete scrambles to pick up the loose money.

DELMAR
Now wuddya suppose is eatin' George?

EVERETT
Well ya know, Delmar, they say that with a thrill-seekin' personality, what goes up must come down. Top of the world one minute, haunted by megrims the next. Yep, it's like our friend George is a alley cat and his own damn humors're swingin' him by the tail. But don't worry, Delmar; he'll be back on top again. I don't think we've heard the last of George Nelson.

Delmar, gazing out at the blackness that has closed over George Nelson, hasn't really been listening. He turns sadly back.

DELMAR
Damn! I liked George.

A FIELD

A ploughing farmer has paused to look for the source of distant string-

band music, growing closer. There is also an approaching amplified voice:

VOICE
Don't be saps for Pappy; vote for Stokes and responsible gummint!

A stakebed truck approaches along the road bordering the field. It is festooned with Stokes banners showing the candidate holding high a broom. Pickers perform in the bed of the truck, along with a dancer doing a two-step as he pushes a broom. A midget in overalls waves his arms, as if conducting the music.

He's against the Innarests and for the little man!

This, the driver's voice, is amplified through a flared speaker mounted on the roof of the cab. As the oncoming truck draws near, the midget bellows out at the farmer, who has removed his hat to scratch his forehead.

MIDGET
Greetings, brother! Vote for Stokes!

The voice tails away:

Clean gummint is yours for the askin'!

Our pan with the passing truck comes to rest on the WEZY radio building.

INSIDE

We are pulling back from a close shot of the portly blind man.

MAN
Hang on! Lemme slap up a wire.

He turns away to load a recording as he talks into a microphone:

Folks, here's my cousin Ezzard's niece Eudora from out Greenwood doin' a little number with her cousin Tom-Tom which I predict you're just gonna enjoy thoroughly.

He switches off the microphone as the song, a duet of 'I'll Fly Away', scratchily issues from a monitor. He turns his attention back to a well-dressed man sitting nearby.

Now what can I do you for, Mister French?

FRENCH
How can I lay hold a the Soggy Bottom Boys?

MAN
Soggy Bottom Boys – I don't precisely recollect, uh –

FRENCH
They cut a record in here, few days ago, old-timey harmony thing with a guitar accump – accump – uh –

MAN
Oh I remember 'em, colored fellas I believe, swell bunch a boys, sung into yon can and skedaddled.

FRENCH
Well that record has just gone through the goddamn roof! They're playin' it as far away as Mobile! The whole damn state's goin' ape!

MAN
It *was* a powerful air.

FRENCH
Hot damn, we gotta find those boys! Sign 'em to a big fat contract! Hell's bells, Mr Lunn, if we don't, the goddamn competition will!

MAN
Oh mercy, yes. You gotta beat that competition.

'I'll Fly Away' mixes up to play full over the following.

MONTAGE

– The three men walk down a flat delta road, the sun shimmering off the rough pavement. Their bank loot, wrapped in a bandana, is knotted to the end of a stick slung over Delmar's shoulder.

– A different road under a threatening sky. The three men stand in the middle distance, waiting. In the foreground two little black boys are walking home, each carrying a block of ice. A horse-drawn cart rumbles in from offscreen and Everett waggles his thumb. Thunder rumbles.

– *A spinning 78 on a green felt turntable. The crude black label identifies it as 'Man of Constant Sorrow' by The Soggy Bottom Boys.*

– *A high shot looking down through the rain past the dripping eave of a barn, under which Everett, Pete and Delmar have taken cover. The three hold their coats pinched shut at the neck as they look forlornly up at the weather.*

– *The three men walk along a red dirt road elevated through a bayou.*

– *The three men sit around a campfire. Everett sits on a stump, expressively telling a ghost story as Pete and Delmar gaze at him from below, wide-eyed and rapt.*

– *The three men walk past a cotton field dotted with burst pods.*

– *A Woolworth's interior. A sad-faced woman in a calico dress addresses the clerk:*

SAD-FACED WOMAN
Do you have the Soggy Bottom Boys performing 'Man of Constant Sorrow'?

CLERK
No, ma'am, we had a new shipment in yesterday but we just can't keep it on the shelves.

The sad-faced woman is crestfallen.

SAD-FACED WOMAN
Oh, mercy. Then – just the purple toilet water.

– *The three men walk down the a road excavated through banks of clay, from which gnarled tree roots protrude.*

– *A pie rests on a windowsill, steam wafting from it. A hand enters from below the sill outside and disappears with the pie. A moment later we see Everett's and Pete's backs as they scamper away across the yard. A short beat, and then Delmar peeks over the sill. He ducks back down and then his hand reaches up to leave a dollar bill. Moments later we see him scampering away after Pete and Everett.*

– *Another campfire. The three men sit around it laughing as they enjoy the pie, each with a slab on a plate improvised of old newspaper. Everett finishes his piece, licks his thumb and tosses the newspaper onto the fire.*

We jump in to look at the soiled newspaper as flame begins to curl its edge. A story is headlined 'TVA Finalizing Plans for Flooding of Arktabutta Valley'. The flame curls the page away, briefly revealing the page beneath – with a story headlined 'Soggy Bottom Boys a Sensation – But Who Are They?' – before it too is consumed.

– A little general store. We are very high, looking down at a foreshortened Everett, Pete, Delmar and store clerk, who is wielding a long telescoping pole that stretches towards us. Everett is pointing up, directing the man with the pole. He moves it tentatively to and fro until, at a certain point, Everett nods vigorously.

A reverse shows the end of the pole – a long stock-pincher – as it closes over a tin of Dapper Dan pomade, resting on a high shelf.

The exterior of the store shows it to be on a corner of a little crossroads town. The three men are emerging from the store just as a car pulls up to one of the two bubble-topped gas pumps out front. A fancyman in a boater hat gets out of the car and heads for the store, passing the three; Everett glances at him and, as the man disappears inside, he dives into his car, waving for Delmar and Pete to follow. Delmar, initially reluctant, is hauled into the car by Pete, and the men take off.

– The spinning 78 recording, as the song enters its last verse.

– A spinning car wheel.

– A panoramic boom up as the car toodles away, down a road that winds through scrub grass toward a distant sunset.

THE CAR

The three men are driving through the heat of the day. Everett drives; Pete is slouched in the front passenger seat; Delmar, in black, picks out 'I'll Fly Away' on a banjo.

Pete listens to something, squints, tilts his head.

PETE
. . . Shutup, Delmar.

Delmar and Everett exchange glances; Everett shrugs and Delmar desists.

We can faintly hear a high, unearthly singing. Barely human, the sound seems to agitate Pete. He looks desperately out the window.

His hinging point-of-view shows, down the declivity from the road and half hidden by trees, three women washing clothes in the river.

Pete's reaction is enormous. He jams a fist into his mouth, eyes widening. He yanks the fist out and screams:

PETE

PULL OVER!

Everett, startled, does so.

EXT.

Before the car has even come to a stop Pete's door flies open and he is stumbling down the bank to the river.

Everett and Delmar follow more casually, Everett chuckling.

EVERETT

I guess ol' Pete's got the itch.

AT THE RIVER

The unearthly singing, full volume here, comes from the three women, beautiful but marked by an otherworldly langor as they dunk clothes in the stream and beat them against rocks.

Pete is all awkward smiles and deep, burning eyes:

PETE

Howdy do, ladies. Name of Pete!

Strangely, the three laundresses do not answer, though they do smile at him as they continue to sing.

Pete tries again as he reaches into their laundry basket:

Maybe I could help you with the, uh –

He realizes he is holding ladies' undergarments.

Ahem. I, uh . . .

He drops them back in the basket.

I don't believe I've, uh, heard that song before . . .

Everett and Delmar have arrived; Everett is loud and jovial:

EVERETT
Aintcha gonna innerduce us, Pete?

Pete's eyes stay glued on the women as he hisses out of the corner of his mouth:

PETE
Don't know their names. I seen 'em first!

Everett laughs lightly.

EVERETT
Ladies, you'll have to pardon my friend here; Pete is dirt-ignorant and unschooled in the social arts. My name on the other hand is Ulysses Everett McGill and you ladies are about the three *prettiest* water lilies it's ever been my privilege to admire.

None of the women respond but, as all continue to sing, one brings a jug marked with three Xes to Everett.

Why, thank you dear, that's very, uh . . .

He takes a swig.

Mm. Corn licker, I guess, uh, the preferred local uh . . .

He passes the jug to Pete as the woman runs her fingers through his hair.

The other two women are approaching to likewise tousle Pete and Delmar.

Delmar's woman caresses his face and, by squeezing his cheeks, smushes his mouth into a pucker.

DELMAR
Pleased to meet you, ma'am.

The singing continues. The stream gurgles. Somewhere, in the distance, flies lazily buzz.

PETE

Damn!

FADE OUT

FADE IN: CLOSE ON DELMAR

We are very tight. Delmar's eyes are closed. We hear loud snoring. At length his eyelids flutter open, but the snoring continues.

Delmar groggily props himself on one elbow.

It is late afternoon. He is still on the riverbank. Everett snores nearby.

The ladies are gone. The hamper of laundry is gone. Pete is gone.

After looking blearily about for a moment, Delmar starts and staggers to his feet.

DELMAR
Holy Saint Christopher!

He toes Everett urgently in the ribs.

EVERETT

Whuhh . . .

DELMAR
Oh sweet Lord, Everett, looka this!

Pete's clothes are laid out on the ground, not in a heap, but mimicking the human shape, as if he had been simply vaporized from within them.

Everett rouses himself and looks at the clothes. He scans the opposite river bank.

EVERETT

PETE! Where the heck are ya! We ain't got time for your shenanigans!

Delmar stares horrified at the pile of clothes: a spot in the middle of the shirt is rising and falling, rising and falling.

DELMAR

Sweet Jesus, Everett! They left his heart!

Everett joins Delmar to look. The rhythmic rising and falling now travels up the shirt. A large yellow toad sticks its head out from under the collar.

Delmar keens. Everett is bewildered.

EVERETT

What on earth is goin' on here! What's got into you, Delmar!

DELMAR

Caintcha see it Everett! Them sigh-reens did this to Pete! They loved him up an' turned him into a horney-toad!

The toad hops down the river bank.

Pete! Come back!

He slides down the bank after the toad, Everett watching in perturbation.

The toad plops into the river and Delmar dives in after him. He emerges a moment later with the toad wriggling in his hand.

Don't worry, Pete! It's me, Delmar! Oh Everett! What're we gonna do?!

DRIVING

We hear soft whimpering as Everett drives, sneaking worried glances over at the passenger seat.

Delmar has the toad in his lap. He whimpers as he pets it.

Everett hesitantly offers:

EVERETT
. . . I'm not sure that's Pete.

DELMAR
Course it's Pete! Look at 'im!

The frog croaks.

We gotta find some kinda wizard can change 'im back!

A beat. Delmar continues to whimper.

Everett squints and shakes his head.

EVERETT
. . . I'm just not sure that's Pete.

FINE RESTAURANT

The tables are formally laid with linen. Delmar and Everett sit at a table, a shoebox between them, deep in conversation.

EVERETT
You can't display a toad in a fine restaurant like this! Why, the good folks here'd go right off their feed!

DELMAR
I just don't think it's right, keepin' him under wraps like we's ashamed of him.

EVERETT
Well if that is Pete I *am* ashamed of him. The way I see it he got what he deserved – fornicating with some whore a Babylon. These things –

He points a knife at the shoebox.

– don't happen for no reason, Delmar. Obviously it's some kind of judgment on Pete's character.

ANOTHER PATRON

We are looking over the shoulder of a broad-shouldered man in a cream-colored suit and a shirt with powder-blue collar. He is digging into a huge plateful of steak and eggs. Sensing something, he looks up, cocks his head, and then slowly turns to look back.

He thus reveals a cream-colored eyepatch with powder-blue trim; his good eye is looking intently off – at Everett and Delmar, who continue arguing, out of earshot.

BACK TO EVERETT AND DELMAR

Still heatedly discussing.

> DELMAR
> The two of *us* was fixing to fornicate!

The waitress has just arrived for their order. Everett gives her an ingratiating laugh:

> EVERETT
> Heh-heh. You'll have to excuse my rusticated friend here, unaccustomed as he is to city manners.

He ostentatiously fans some of his money.

> Well mamzel I guess we'll have a couple a steaks and some gratinated potatoes and wash it down with your finest bubbly wine –

BIG MAN

Watching Everett fan his money. The big man stops chewing and slowly raises his napkin to his lips to give them a dainty pat.

BACK TO EVERETT AND DELMAR

As Everett closes his menu.

> EVERETT
> . . . And I don't suppose the chef'd have any nits or grubs in the pantry, or – naw, never mind, just bring me a couple leafs a raw cabbage.

WAITRESS

Yes sir.

The big man appears as she leaves.

BIG MAN

Don't believe I've seen you boys around here before! Allow
me t'innerduce myself: name of Daniel Teague, known in
these precincts as Big Dan Teague or, to those who're
pressed for time, Big Dan toot cort.

EVERETT

How d'you do, Big Dan. I'm Ulysses Everett McGill; this is
my associate Delmar O'Donnell. I sense that, like me, you are
endowed with the gift of gab.

Big Dan chuckles as he draws up a chair.

BIG DAN

I flatter myself that such is the case; in my line of work it's
plumb necessary. The one thing you don't want is air in the
conversation.

EVERETT

Once again we find ourselves in agreement. What kind of
work you do, Big Dan?

BIG DAN

Sales, Mr McGill, sales! And what do I sell? The Truth! Ever'
blessed word of it, from Genesee on down to Revelations!
That's right, the word of God, which let me add there is
damn good money in during these days of woe and want!
Folks're lookin' for answers and Big Dan Teague sells the
only book that's got 'em! What do *you* do – you and your, uh,
tongue-tied friend?

DELMAR

Uh, we uh –

EVERETT

We're adventurers, sir, currently pursuin' a certain
opportunity but open to others as well.

BIG DAN

I like your style, young man, so I'm gonna propose you a
proposition. You cover my check so I don't have to run back
up to my room, have your waitress wrap your dinner picnic-
style, and we'll retire to more private environs where I will
explain to you how vast amounts of money can be made in
the service of God Amighty.

Everett rises and digs in his pocket.

EVERETT

Well, why not. If nothing else I could use some civilized
conversation.

*As the three men start to move off, Big Dan gives Delmar a tilt of the
head and a crinkling smile.*

BIG DAN

Don't forget your shoebox, friend.

We hear bellowing issuing from a curtained private dining-room.

INSIDE THE PRIVATE ROOM

*Pappy O'Daniel sits smoking a cigar, nursing a glass of whiskey, and
soliciting the counsel of his overweight retinue.*

PAPPY

Languishing! Goddamn campaign is languishing! We need a
shot inna arm! Hear me, boys? Inna goddamn ARM!
Election held tomorra, that sonofabitch Stokes would win it
in a walk!

JUNIOR

Well he's the reform candidate, Daddy.

Pappy narrows his eyes at him, wondering what he's getting at.

PAPPY

. . . Yeah?

JUNIOR

Well people like that reform. Maybe we should get us some.

Pappy whips off his hat and slaps at Junior with it.

PAPPY

I'll reform you, you soft-headed sonofabitch! How we gonna run reform when we're the damn incumbent!

He glares around the table.

Zat the best idea any you boys can come up with? REEform?! Weepin' Jesus on the cross! Eckard, you may as well start draftin' my concession speech right now.

Eckard grunts as he starts to rise:

ECKARD

Okay, Pappy.

Pappy whips him back down with his hat.

PAPPY

I'm just makin' a point, you stupid sonofabitch!

ECKARD

Okay, Pappy.

As he settles back Eckard looks around the table and helpfully relays:

Pappy just makin' a point here, boys.

A MEADOW

The car boosted from the general store has been pulled off the road and parked a few yards into a field littered with bluebonnets and rimmed by moss-dripping oak.

Everett, Delmar and Big Dan sit on a blanket around a large picnic hamper. Big Dan is just sucking the last piece of chicken off a bone.

He tosses the bone over his shoulder, belches, and sighs.

BIG DAN
Thankee boys for throwin' in that fricassee. I'm a man a large appetites and even with lunch under my belt I was feeling a mite peckish.

EVERETT
Our pleasure, Big Dan.

BIG DAN
And thank you as well for that conversational hiatus; I generally refrain from speech while engaged in gustation. There are those who attempt both at the same time but I find it coarse and vulgar. Now where were we?

DELMAR
Makin' money in the Lord's service.

BIG DAN
You don't say much friend, but when you do it's to the point and I salute you for it.

Delmar is pleased and embarrassed.

DELMAR
Oh, it weren't nothin', I –

BIG DAN
Yes, Bible sales. The trade is not a complicated one; there're but two things to learn. One bein' where to find your wholesaler – word of God in bulk as it were. Two bein' how to reckanize your customer – who're you dealin' with? – an exercise in psychology so to speak.

He rises to his feet and tosses down his napkin.

57

And it is that which I propose to give you a lesson in right now.

He reaches up and with one hand easily rips a stout limb off a tree. He casually strips its twigs.

EVERETT
I like to think that I'm a pretty astute observer of the human scene.

BIG DAN
No doubt, brother – I figured as much back there in the restaurant. That's why I invited you out here for this advanced tutorial.

His club is ready. He swings it at Delmar who staggers back with a grunt.

Everett wears a puzzled smile.

EVERETT
. . . What's goin' on, Big Dan?

Delmar, though stunned, is faster to size things up. He charges Big Dan and wraps his arms around him.

Delmar roars.

Big Dan roars back and whacks at his head.

Everett is still puzzled, but willing to be instructed:

>Big Dan, what're you doin'?

Big Dan walks awkwardly over to Everett with Delmar still attached to him like a hunting dog locked on to a bear. Big Dan takes a break from whacking at Delmar to deliver a blow to Everett.

The blow catches Everett on the chin and sends him reeling.

BIG DAN
>It's all about money, boys! Atsy answer! Dough re mi!

Big Dan bear hugs Delmar and tosses him away. He whacks Everett into a semi-conscious heap and then paws through his pockets.

>Do unto others before they do unto you!

He pulls out their wad of cash.

>I'll just take your show cards . . .

He walks over to Delmar who is on the ground moaning, and kicks him several times.

>. . . and whatever you got in the hole.

He takes Delmar's shoebox and flips off the top.

Inside is a bed of straw with the toad resting on it.

>What the . . .

He pokes around the straw with his finger; nothing else inside.

>It's nothin' but a damn toad!

Delmar, moaning, looks blearily up through swollen eyes.

Big Dan has the toad in his enormous fist.

Delmar moans through cracked and bloody lips:

DELMAR
>No . . . you don't understand . . .

Don't you boys know these things give ya warts?

He squeezes the frog, crushing it, and tosses it away against a tree.

DELMAR

Oh Lord . . . Pete . . .

Big Dan is over at the car, cranking it up.

BIG DAN

End of lesson.

He climbs in.

So long, boys! Hee-hee! See ya in the funny papers!

The car belches and pops and toodles off down the road.

Delmar staggers to his feet and stumbles over to the carcass of the frog, weeping.

DELMAR

Pete . . . Pete . . . Pete . . .

FADE OUT

PAN DOWN FROM BLACK TO BRING IN A TORCH

Flickering in the night. We hear the rumble of distant thunder as the continued pan down brings the torch's bearer into frame – a man with the slavering grin of the dim-witted sadist. He watches as we hear:

VOICE

Where are they?!

There is the sound of a lash and a scream.

Talk, you unreconstructed whelp of a whore! Where they headed?

Another lash brings another scream.

The screams come from Pete. His arms, stretched high over his head, are tied to a tree limb. His interrogator wields a bullwhip.

INTERROGATOR

Your screams ain't gonna save your flesh! Only your tongue is, boy!

Another lash, another scream.

Where they headed!

A third man walks into the torchlight, a hound drooling at his heels. He is Cooley, the sheriff with mirrored sunglasses whom we remember from previous barn confrontations.

COOLEY

Lump. I.O.

The two men acknowledge by backing away from Pete.

We hear a pat . . . pat . . . and then the accelerating pitter-patter of arriving rain.

Cooley looks up.

Sweet summer rain. Like God's own mercy.

He looks back down at Pete.

Your two friends have abandoned you, Pete. They don't seem to care 'bout your hide.

He shrugs, looks off.

. . . Okay.

Looking up, into black: a rope is tossed up – it recedes out of the torchlight into black night – and then drops back down into the light, a noose bouncing at its end.

Stairway to heaven, Pete.

The two henchmen fit the noose over Pete's neck. Cooley licks his lips. His dog slobbers.

We shall all meet, by and by.

PETE

Goddamnit!

Cooley holds up one hand. The two men pause in fitting the noose.

Pete is sobbing:

Godfer gimme!

Thunder crashes.

BACK OF A HAYTRUCK

Everett and Delmar sit disconsolately on a haybale as the stakebed truck bounces along a rough country road. They are both ill-kempt and heavily bruised.

Though still an undammable river of verbiage, Everett now seems to be talking out of weary habit, not conviction:

EVERETT

Believe me, Delmar, he would've wanted us to press on. Pete, rest his soul, was one sour-assed sonofabitch and not given to acts of pointless sentimentality.

Delmar doggedly shakes his head.

DELMAR

It just don't seem right, diggin' up that treasure without him.

We distantly hear picks ringing and male chanting. Hollow-eyed, Everett tries to convince himself as much as Delmar:

EVERETT

Maybe it's for the best that Pete was squushed. Why, he was barely a sentient bein'. Now, soon as we clean ourselves up, get a little smell'um in our hair, we're just gonna feel a hunnert per cent better about ourselves and about . . .

His voice trails away as he looks out at the road.

They are passing a line of chained men in prison stripes and duck-billed caps wielding pickaxes and shovels at the side of the road. Guards bearing shotguns amble back and forth.

As he stares at the line of men Everett tries to pick up his thread:

. . . and about . . . life in general . . .

The prisoners look like phantoms in the heat and dust.

Jesus. We must be near Parchman Farm.

The men, giving throat to a dolorous chain-gang chant, do not look up at the passing haytruck.

Everett is haunted:

Sorry sonsabitches . . . Seems like a year ago we bust off the farm . . .

The last man in line swings his pick and, as he grows smaller, looks up. Everett stares.

It is Pete.

Lone and lorn, he returns Everett's slack-jawed stare until heat ripples and the truck's dusty wake dissolve him away.

Everett blinks.

Pete have a brother?

DELMAR

Not that I'm aware.

Everett shakes his head as if to clear it.

EVERETT

. . . Heat must be gettin' to me.

The truck rattles on.

TOWN SQUARE

Ithaca, Mississippi. On a bunting-covered stage a pencil-necked man with round rimless glasses addresses a crowd of rustics.

The pencil-neck is identified on posters as 'Homer Stokes, Friend of the Little Man', and, in life as in the pictures, he shakes a broom over his head. A midget in overalls stands next to him.

STOKES

And I say to you that the great state a Mississippi cannot *afford* four more years a Pappy O'Daniel – four more years a cronyism, nepotism, rascalism and service to the Innarests!

63

The choice, she's a clear 'un: Pappy O'Daniel, *slave* a the Innarests; Homer Stokes, *servant* a the little man! Ain't that right, little fella?

The midget enthusiastically seconds:

MIDGET

He ain't lyin'!

STOKES

When the little man says jump, Homer Stokes says how high? And, ladies'n jettymens, the little man has admonished me to grasp the broom a ree-form and sweep this state clean!

The midget waves his little midget broom in time with Stokes's waves.

It's gonna be back to the flour mill, Pappy! The Innarests can take care a theyselves! Come Tuesday, we gonna sweep the rascals out! Clean gummint – yours for the askin'!

He beams amid cheers and then, as three girls in gingham frocks run out to join him:

An' now – the little Wharvey gals! Whatcha got for us, darlin's?

The oldest girl is about ten.

LITTLE GIRL

'In the Highways'!

STOKES

That's fine.

The haytruck has pulled into the square and Everett and Delmar are climbing out.

Everett stares at the stage.

EVERETT

Wharvey gals?! Did he just say the little *Wharvey* gals?

Delmar shrugs. For some reason, Everett is enraged:

God*damnit* all!

Onstage, the three girls are singing in untrained but enthusiastic harmony:

GIRLS
In the highways
In the hedges . . .

Everett stomps toward the stage, fighting his way through the crowd. Puzzled, Delmar follows.

DELMAR
You know them gals, Everett?

Everett reaches the stage and climbs up into the wings just as the song ends. The midget starts buck-dancing to a fiddle tune as the three little girls, filing off, notice Everett.

YOUNGEST
Daddy!

MIDDLE
He ain't our daddy!

EVERETT
Hell I ain't! Whatsis 'Wharvey' gals? – Your name's McGill!

YOUNGEST
No sir! Not since you got hit by a train!

EVERETT
What're you talkin' about – I wasn't hit by a train!

MIDDLE
Mama said you was hit by a train!

YOUNGEST
Blooey!

OLDEST
Nothin' left!

MIDDLE
Just a grease spot on the L&N!

EVERETT
Damnit, I never been hit by any train!

OLDEST

At's right! So Mama's got us back to Wharvey!

MIDDLE

That's a maiden name.

YOUNGEST

You got a maiden name, Daddy?

EVERETT

No, Daddy ain't got a maiden name; ya see –

MIDDLE

That's your misfortune!

YOUNGEST

At's right! And now Mama's got a new beau!

OLDEST

He's a suitor!

EVERETT

Yeah, I know 'bout that.

MIDDLE

Mama says he's bona fide!

This worries Everett:

EVERETT

Hm. He give her a ring?

YOUNGEST

Yassir, big'un!

MIDDLE

Gotta gem!

OLDEST

Mama checked it!

YOUNGEST

It's bona fide!

MIDDLE

He's a suitor!

Hm. What's his name?

MIDDLE

Vernon T. Waldrip.

YOUNGEST

Uncle Vernon.

OLDEST

Till tomorrow.

YOUNGEST

Then he's gonna be Daddy!

EVERETT

I'm the only daddy you got! *I'm* the damn paterfamilias!

OLDEST

Yeah, but you ain't bona fide!

EVERETT

Hm. Where's your mama?

Stokes is announcing from the stage:

STOKES

And now let's fetch back the Wharvey gals to sing 'I'll Fly Away'.

The girls call over their shoulders as they run back onstage:

MIDDLE

She's at the five and dime.

YOUNGEST

Buyin' nipples!

WOOLWORTH'S

The faces of a six-year-old girl and her four-year-old sister light up.

GIRLS

Daddy!

Next to them is a two-year-old girl with a string wrapped round her

*waist. The other end of the string is held by a woman in her thirties with
a haggard, careworn face. The woman also holds a babe-in-arms.*

Everett, entering, goggles at the infant.

EVERETT

Who the hell is that?!

WOMAN

Starla Wharvey.

EVERETT

Starla McGill you mean! How come you never told me about
her?

SIX-YEAR-OLD

'Cause you was hit by a train.

EVERETT

And that's another thing – why're you tellin' our gals I was hit
by a train!

WOMAN

Lotta respectable people been hit by trains. Judge Hobby over
in Cookeville was hit by a train. What was I supposed to tell

'em – that you was sent to the penal farm and I divorced you
from shame?

EVERETT
Well – I take your point. But it leaves me in a damned
awkward position *vis-à-vis* my progeny.

A man in a straw boater joins them.

BOATER
'Lo Penny . . . This gentleman bothering you?

EVERETT
You Waldrip?

BOATER
That's right.

Everett sniffs and, catching a scent, squints.

*Waldrip's hair, protruding from under his boater, is plastered against
his scalp.*

EVERETT
. . . Have you been using my hair treatment?

WALDRIP
Your hair treatment?!

Everett covers his anger with an exaggerated politeness:

EVERETT
S'cuse me . . .

He draws Penny aside.

Well, I got news for you case you hadn't noticed – I *wasn't* hit
by a train. And I've traveled many a weary mile to be back
with my wife and six daughters.

SIX-YEAR-OLD
Seven, Daddy!

PENNY
That ain't your daddy, Alvinelle. Your daddy was hit by a
train.

EVERETT

Now Penny, stop that!

PENNY

No – you stop it! Vernon here's got a job. Vernon's got prospects. He's bona fide! What're *you*?

EVERETT

I'll tell you what I am – I'm the paterfamilias! You can't marry *him*!

PENNY

I can and I am and I will – tomorrow! I gotta think about the little Wharvey gals! They look to *me* for answers! Vernon can s'port 'em and buy 'em lessons on the clarinet! The only good thing *you* ever did for the gals was get hit by that train!

EVERETT

. . . Why you . . . lyin' . . . unconstant . . . succubus!

WALDRIP

You can't swear at my fiancée!

EVERETT

Oh yeah? Well you can't marry my *wife*!

With this he takes a wild swing which Waldrip easily eludes. Waldrip adapts a Marquess of Queensbury stance and prances about, delivering stinging punches to the nose of a stunned and outclassed Everett.

A crowd is gathering and voices murmur:

BYSTANDERS

Who is that man?

PENNY

He's not my husband. Just a drifter, I guess . . . Just some no-account drifter . . .

EXT. WOOLWORTH'S

Its glass doors swing open and Everett is hurled out and bellyflops into the dust of the street.

BRAWNY MANAGER

. . . And stay out of Woolworth's!

MOVIE THEATER

Romantic music tinnily plays as Delmar and Everett watch, Everett slumped down and angrily hissing:

EVERETT

Deceitful! *Two*-faced! *She*-Woman! *Never* trust a female, Delmar! Remember that one simple precept and your time with me will not have been ill spent!

DELMAR

Okay, Everett.

EVERETT

Hit by a train! Truth means nothin' to Woman, Delmar. Triumph a the subjective! You ever been with a woman?

DELMAR

Well, uh, I – I gotta get the family farm back before I can start thinkin' about *that.*

73

EVERETT

Well that's right! If then! Believe me, Delmar, Woman is the most fiendish instrument of torture ever devised to bedevil the days a man!

DELMAR

Everett, I never figured you for a paterfamilias.

EVERETT

Oh-ho-ho yes, I've spread my seed. And you see what it, uh . . . what it's earned me . . . Now what in the . . .

The screen is flickering down to black as the music slows to sludge and stops.

The theater is dark and quiet.

Everett and Delmar, and the rest of the sparse audience, look restively about.

A man carrying a shotgun enters the auditorium.

He walks halfway down the aisle and stops several rows behind Delmar and Everett. He scans the theater, then brings a whistle to his lips.

At his whistle the back doors burst open and a line of chained men trot in at double-time. With much clanking they file into one row and then, that row filled, the one behind it. They remain silently on their feet.

The first guard and two others who escorted in the convicts scan the theater. The first guard again blows his whistle.

The two rows of chained men sit.

After another silence:

FIRST GUARD

. . . Okay boys! Enjoy yer pickcha show!

One more whistle cues the movie to grind back up to speed.

A hissing whisper from behind draws Everett and Delmar's attention:

VOICE

Do not seek the treasure! It's a bushwhack!

Everett and Delmar turn and stare, saucer-eyed. In the middle of the frontmost row of convicts sits Pete – bald, haunted Pete.

After a long, disbelieving stare:

DELMAR
. . . Pete?

Pete whispers again, urgently:

PETE
They're fixin' a ambush! Do not seek the treasure!

Everett, jaw hanging open, can only stare, as if at a ghost. Delmar stares also, but finally brings out another:

DELMAR
. . . Pete?

PETE
Do not seek the treasure!

Everett's face remains frozen in horrified disbelief, but Delmar finally accepts Pete's corporeal reality.

DELMAR
We thought you was a toad!

Pete squints and cocks his head as if to say, What was that?

Delmar repeats the whisper slowly and with exaggerated mouth movements:

We *thought* . . . you *was* . . . a *toad*!

Pete shakes his head – didn't catch it – and repeats, also overarticulating:

PETE
Do *not* . . . *seek* . . . the *treasure*!

A guard murmurs:

GUARD
Quiet there. Watcha pickcha.

VERANDA

Pappy O'Daniel sits on the veranda of the Governor's Mansion, smoking a cigar and sipping from a glass of bourbon as the evening sun goes down.

PAPPY

I signed that bill! I signed a dozen a those aggi-culture bills! Everyone knows I'm a friend a the fahmuh! What do I gotta do, start diddlin' livestock?!

JUNIOR

We cain't do that, Daddy, we might offend our constichency.

PAPPY

We ain't *got* a constichency! *Stokes* got a constichency!

ECKARD

Them straw polls is ugly.

SPIVEY

Stokes is pullin' ah pants down.

ECKARD

Gonna pluck us off the tit.

SPIVEY

Pappy gonna be sittin' there pants down and *Stokes* at the table soppin' up the gravy.

ECKARD

Latch right *on* to that tit.

SPIVEY

Wipin' little circles with his bread.

ECKARD

Suckin' away.

SPIVEY

Well, it's a well-run campaign, midget'n broom'n whatnot.

ECKARD

Devil his due.

SPIVEY

Helluva awgazation.

JUNIOR

Say, I gotten idee.

ECKARD

What sat, Junior?

JUNIOR

We could hire us a little fella even smaller'n Stokes's.

Pappy whips at him with his hat.

PAPPY

Y' ignorant slope-shouldered sack a guts! Why we'd look like
a buncha satchel-ass Johnnie-Come-Latelies braggin' on our
own midget! Don't matter how stumpy! And that's the
goddamn problem right there – people think this Stokes got
fresh ideas, he's oh coorant and we the past.

ECKARD

Problem a p'seption.

SPIVEY

Ass right.

ECKARD

Reason why he's pullin' ah pants down.

SPIVEY

Gonna paddle ah little bee-hind.

ECKARD

Ain't gonna paddle it; he's gonna *kick* it real hard.

*With his mouth forming an O around his drooping cigar, Pappy looks
sadly from one to the other, like a spectator at a particularly boring
tennis match.*

SPIVEY

No, I believe he's a-gonna paddle it.

ECKARD

Well now, I don't believe assa property scription.

77

SPIVEY

Well, that's how I characterize it.

ECKARD

Well, I believe it's mawva kickin' sichation.

SPIVEY

Pullin' ah pants down . . .

ECKARD

Wipin' little circles with his bread . . .

A NOOSE

In slow motion it is dropping . . . dropping . . . dropping through the night. We hear distant thunder and the howl of a hound. The sounds recede, and the black background dissolves into a pan down from a raftered ceiling as the noose fades away.

The continued pan down shows that we are in a barracks-like cabin. It is night. Convicts are ranged in bunk-beds. Their snores stand out against the chirr of crickets.

In the upper berth of the foreground bed is Pete. His hands are clasped behind his head. A manacle and chain links one wrist to a rail that serves as headboard.

He stares up, haunted, at the phantom noose.

PETE

I could not gaze upon that far shore . . .

He reacts quizzically to a whispered:

VOICE

Pete!

A moment later Everett rises over the lip of his bed. His face is blacked and he sways as if standing on a boat.

Hold still.

He is raising a large, long-armed, short-nosed pincering tool. He locks the nose onto Pete's chain and levers the arms. As his hand chinks free, Pete does not react to his newfound liberty.

78

We hear an agonized voice from off as Everett continues to sway:

DELMAR

. . . Cain't stand much longer.

Pete's eyes burn into Everett's.

PETE

It was a moment a weakness!

EVERETT

Quitcha babblin' Pete – time to skedaddle.

THE THREE MEN

*We track with them as they walk through the moonlit woods. Delmar's
and Everett's faces are thoroughly blacked; Pete is just finishing
blacking his, and he hands the shoe polish back to Everett.*

PETE

They lured me out for a bathe, then they dunked me 'n
trussed me up like a hog and turned me in for the bounty.

EVERETT

I shoulda guessed it – typical womanly behavior. Just lucky we
left before they came for us.

DELMAR

We didn't abandon you, Pete, we just thought you was a
toad.

PETE

No, they never did turn me into a toad.

DELMAR

Well that was our mistake then. And then we was beat up by a
Bible salesman and banished from Woolworth's. I don't know
if it's the one branch or all of 'em.

PETE

Well I – I ain't had it easy either, boys. Uh, frankly, I – well I
spilled my guts about the treasure.

DELMAR

Huh?!

PETE

Awful sorry I betrayed you fellas; must be my Hogwallop blood.

EVERETT

Aw, that's all right, Pete.

Pete is shaking his head, miserable.

PETE

It's awful white of ya to take it like that, Everett. I feel wretched, spoilin' yer play for a million dollars'n point two. It's been eatin' at my guts.

EVERETT

Aw, that's all right.

Pete starts weeping.

PETE

You boys're true friends!

He hugs a stunned Delmar.

You're m'boon companions!

He hugs Everett, who looks profoundly uncomfortable.

EVERETT

Pete, uh, I don't want ya to beat yourself up about this thing . . .

PETE

I cain't help it, but that's a wonderful thing to say!

EVERETT

Well, but Pete . . .

He clears his throat.

Uh, the fact of the matter is – well, damnit, there *ain't* no treasure!

Now it is Pete's turn to be stunned. He and Delmar stare at Everett.

Fact of the matter – there never was!

PETE

But . . . but . . .

DELMAR

So – where's all the money from your armored-car job?

EVERETT

I never knocked over any armored-car. I was sent up for practicing law without a license.

PETE

But . . .

EVERETT

Damnit, I just hadda bust out! My wife wrote me she was gettin' married! I gotta stop it!

Pete stares vacantly off.

PETE

. . . No treasure . . . I had two weeks left on my sentence . . .

EVERETT

I couldn't wait two weeks! She's gettin' married tomorra!

PETE

. . . With my added time for the escape, I don't get out now 'til 1987 . . . I'll be eighty-four years old.

Delmar, not angry himself, is trying to work it out.

DELMAR

Huh. I guess they'll tack on fifty years for me too.

EVERETT

Boys, we was chained together. I hadda tell ya *some*thin'. Bustin' out alone was not a option!

PETE

. . . Eighty-four years old.

Delmar brightens:

DELMAR

I'll only be eighty-two.

Pete lunges at Everett.

PETE

YOU RUINED MY LIFE!

He tackles him and, with his hands wrapped round Everett's throat, the two roll over.

EVERETT
(strangled)

Pete . . . I do apologize.

PETE

Eighty-four years old! I'll be gummin' pab-you-lum!

They have rolled through some brush and their bodies are now halfway into a clearing. They abruptly stop.

Pete, lying on top of Everett, looks up, startled by loud chanting. Everett, lying on his back, tries to see as well, his eyes rolling back in his head.

Their point-of-view shows a great open field where men in bedsheets parade in formation before a huge fiery cross.

Pete and Everett hastily crabwalk back into the bushes and then peek through with Delmar.

The ranks of hooded men, chanting in a high hillbilly wail, intersect and shuffle like a marching band at halftime. At length they stop in perfect formation, still chanting, to face the Imperial Wizard, who stands in front of the burning cross dressed in a red satin robe and hood trimmed with gold.

An aisle leads through the middle of the formation to the burning cross, before which a gibbet has been erected. The backmost row has stopped, facing away, only a few yards from the bushes that hide Delmar, Pete and Everett.

As the chanting continues, two Klansmen lead a black man, whom they grasp by either arm, up the aisle toward the gibbet.

> BLACK MAN
> I ain't never harmed any you gentlemen!

Everett hisses:

> EVERETT
> It's Tommy! They got Tommy!

> DELMAR
> Oh my God!

It is indeed Tommy Johnson.

> TOMMY
> I ain't never harmed nobody!

Pete is staring aghast at the makeshift gibbet.

> PETE
> The noose. Sweet Jesus! We gotta save 'im!

A broad-shouldered man in the middle of the ranks of Klansmen, sensing something, slowly turns to look back over his shoulder. He thus reveals that his hood has only one eye-hole.

He slowly draws off the hood. It is, of course, Big Dan Teague. His one good eye looks about; his other eye, now revealed, is hideously clouded and stares up and off in fixed sightlessness.

Everett, still crouched behind the bushes, notices something. He hisses and points.

EVERETT

The color guard.

Off to one side is a robed and hooded three-man color guard displaying a Confederate flag.

In front of the crowd the Imperial Wizard raises one satin-draped arm, and the chanting stops.

WIZARD

Brothers! We are foregathered here to preserve our hallowed culture'n heritage! From intrusions, inclusions and dilutions! Of culluh! Of creed! Of our ol'-time religion!

Over in the bushes Everett, Delmar and Pete are straightening up and adjusting their appropriated robes and hoods, having disposed of the color guard.

We aim to pull evil up by the root! Before it chokes out the flower of our culture'n heritage! And our women! Let's not forget those ladies, y'all, lookin' to us for p'tection! From darkies! From Jews! From Papists! And from all those smart-ass folk say we come descended from the monkeys! That's not *my* culture'n heritage!

A roar from the crowd.

Izzat *your* culture'n heritage?

Another roar.

And so . . . we gonna hang us a neegra!

A huge roar – and now the ranks resume their chanting.

The color guard hustles up the aisle to draw up behind the two men leading Tommy to the gibbet. Everett hisses:

EVERETT

Hey Tommy! It's us!

Behind Everett in the deep background someone emerges from the ranks into the middle aisle. He approaches with a strong, purposeful stride – Big Dan Teague, bareheaded, holding his hood under his arm.

Everett hisses again:

Hey Tommy!

Tommy looks back over his shoulder.

TOMMY

. . . Huh?

Everett is oblivious to the big man approaching from behind.

EVERETT

It's us! We come to rescue ya!

TOMMY

That's mighty kind of ya boys, but I don't think nothin's gonna save me now – the devil's come to collect his due!

PETE

Tommy, you don't wanna get hanged!

TOMMY

Naw I don't guess I do, but that's the way it seems to be workin' out.

EVERETT

Listen to me, Tommy, I got a plan –

Whoosh – arriving Big Dan whips the hood from Everett's head. Everett is exposed – in blackface.

The chanting abruptly stops. The crowd is stunned.

Big Dan whips off the other two hoods – Delmar and Pete, in blackface.

From the crowd:

VOICE

The color guard is colored!

Big Dan roars.

The crowd roars.

Everett screams:

EVERETT

Run, boys!

Pandemonium breaks out, and the Imperial Wizard takes off his red satin hood for a better view.

He is the reform candidate Homer Stokes. Next to him, his midget also pulls off his midget hood.

Stokes is peeved.

STOKES

Who made them the color guard?

Everett, Pete, Tommy and Delmar, bearing the Confederate flag, are retreating across the neutral ground separating the mob of Klansmen from the burning cross. The mob pursues in full cry.

When the intruders reach the foot of the cross, Delmar turns. He javelins the flagpole up and out toward the pursuing crowd.

Homer Stokes is mortified:

Damn! Can't let that flag touch the ground!

The crowd gasps and watches, heads tilted back, in silence.

The only sound is the fluttering flag.

Homer Stokes' eyes rise, hesitate and start to fall as the flag reaches its zenith and starts to descend.

We boom down with the hurtling flag toward a sea of upturned white hoods. Dead in the middle is bareheaded Dan Teague.

His arms are tensed out at his sides like a waiting kick-off returner. He squints up with his one good eye, judging distance and trajectory.

From somewhere we hear a loud BOINK, as of a wire popping.

The flag flutters.

The crowd is silent.

Big Dan sets and . . .

WHAP! He snaps his hands up and together.

He has caught the flagpole. The flag has not touched the ground.

The crowd cheers.

Big Dan looks around, beaming acknowledgement of the cheers.

From somewhere, another BOINK.

As Big Dan's look reaches front again, his smile fades.

His eye tracks up – up –

CREEEEEEK! – The fiery cross is twisting and starting to fall.

At the foot of the cross Everett snaps its last guy wire with his pincers – BOINK – and the four men sprint off.

WHOOOOSH – As the crowd scatters, the cross descends toward Big Dan, frozen, looking up.

It crashes in a shower of sparks and embers that obliterates Big Dan Teague.

A PACKARD

It is pulling up in front of a town hall from which party sounds filter out.

Pappy O'Daniel emerges from the car with his retinue – Eckard, Spivey and Junior.

> PAPPY
> I'm sayin' we har this man away.

> ECKARD
> Assa good idea, Pappy.

> SPIVEY
> Helluva idea.

> ECKARD
> Cain't beat 'em, join 'em.

> SPIVEY
> Have *him* join *us*, run *our* campaign 'stead a that pencil-neck's.

> ECKARD
> Enticements a power, wealth, settera.

> SPIVEY
> No one says no to Pappy O'Daniel.

87

Oh gracious no. Not with *his* blandishments.

SPIVEY

Powas p'suasion.

PAPPY

What's his name again?

ECKARD

Campaign manager? Waldrip.

SPIVEY

Vernon Waldrip.

ECKARD

Vernon *T.* Waldrip.

PAPPY

Hmm . . . His folks from out Tuscarora?

SPIVEY

Tuscarora? Might be. I b'lieve they is.

ECKARD

Not a doubt in my mind.

Pappy is disgusted:

PAPPY

You don't know where his goddamn folks from; you speakin'
outcha asshole.

ECKARD

Well now Pappy I wouldn't put it that strong . . .

As the three men make their way up the steps, Eckard's voice is fading:

. . . but p'haps yaw right . . .

In wide shot, they disappear into the building.

*A reverse shows the wide shot to have been the point-of-view of Everett,
Pete, Delmar and Tommy, who peek out from the mouth of an alley.
Everett hisses his intelligence:*

EVERETT

Well, it's a invitation-only affair; we'll have to sneak in
through the service entrance –

PETE

Wait a minute – who elected you leader a this outfit? Since we
been followin' your lead we got nothin' but trouble! I gotten
this close to bein' strung up, 'n consumed in a fire, 'n
whipped no end, 'n sunstroked, 'n soggied –

DELMAR

'N turned into a frog –

EVERETT

He was never turned *in*to a frog!

Delmar sulks:

DELMAR

Almost loved up though.

Everett is stunned.

EVERETT

So you're against me now, too! . . . Is that how it is, boys?

Silence. No one wants to meet Everett's eye. He is saddened.

The whole world and God Almighty . . . and now you. Well,
maybe I deserve this. Boys, I . . . I know I've made some
tactical mistakes. But if you'll just stick with me; I need your
help. And I've *got* a plan. Believe me, boys, we can fix this
thing! I can get my wife back! We can get outta here!

Headlights play; the men suck back into the alley as a car passes by.

*The car tools up to the banquet hall and Homer Stokes emerges with his
midget. The midget tosses his balled-up white hood into the car and both
men shrug into their suitcoats.*

Stokes is angry:

STOKES

. . . goddamn disgrace. Made a travesty of the entire
evenin' . . .

They too start up the stairs. Stokes's pace is brisk and the midget hops awkwardly to keep up.

. . . what I wouldn't give to get my hands on those agitators. Whoever heard a such behavior. Even among culluds. Or mulattos, maybe – I suspect some miscegenation in their heritage . . . how else you goin' explain it – usin' the Confed'it flag as a missile . . .

BANQUET HALL KITCHEN

Everett, Pete, Delmar and Tommy are entering through the back door. The blackface has been scrubbed off but all four now wear long gray beards as disguise, clumsily affixed with spirit gum. Each is carrying a musical-instrument case.

They elbow past the bustling kitchen help.

EVERETT
Scuse me . . . scuse me . . . we're the next act . . .

DELMAR
Everett, my beard itches.

PETE
This is crazy. No one's ever gonna believe we're a real band.

EVERETT
No, this is gonna work! I just gotta get close enough to talk to her. Takin' off with us is got a lot more future in it than marrying a guy named Waldrip. *I'm* goddamn bona fide. *I've got* the answers!

HEAD TABLE

Out in the banquet hall Penny and Waldrip sit side-by-side at the head table, surrounded by the Wharvey gals. Penny and Waldrip are facing the hall with their backs to the stage as the four bearded band members – Everett, Pete, Delmar and Tommy – take their places.

Pappy O'Daniel stands by Waldrip's chair with an arm draped over his shoulder, leaning in to murmur confidentially. Waldrip sits stiffly erect as he listens, frowning at a spot in space.

Suddenly Waldrip erupts:

WALDRIP
Well that's a improper suggestion! I can't switch sides in the middle of a campaign! Especially to work for a man who lacks moral fibre!

PAPPY
Moral fibre?!

He waves his cane, outraged.

You pasty-faced sonofabitch, I *invented* moral fibre!

Up on the stage, the band has launched into a song.

Pappy O'Daniel was displayin' rectitude and high-mindedness when that pencil-neck *you* work for was still messin' his drawers!

A hissed:

VOICE
Pssst! Penny! Hey! Up here!

As the two men continue to exchange sharp words, Penny turns her head to look steeply up over her shoulder.

Everett is up onstage just behind her. As the rest of the band continues to play, he is parting his beard to hiss down at her:

Penny! It's me!

Dismayed, she shakes her head and tries to unobtrusively wave him away. He is undeterred:

No, Penny, listen! We're leavin' the state! Pursuin' opportunities in another venue! I got big plans! Not minstrelsy; this-here's just a dodge – I'm gonna be a dentist! I know a guy who'll print me up a license! I wanna be what you want me to be, honey! I want you and the gals to come with me!

She shakes her head vigorously and looks down at her plate as Everett continues pleading to her back:

They're my daughters, Penny! *I'm* the king a *this* goddamn castle!

Stokes has ambled up to the head table.

STOKES
What're you doin' here, Pappy? I guess someone let on there was free liquor, heh-heh.

PAPPY
Yeah, you'll be laughin' out the other side your face come November.

ECKARD
Pappy O'*Daniel* be laughin' then.

SPIVEY
Not out the other side his face, though.

ECKARD
Oh no, no, just the reg'la side –

This byplay is interrupted by a roar from the crowd.

The band has launched into 'Man of Constant Sorrow', precipitating the huge reaction. Everett, still trying to get Penny's attention, looks up, stunned at the ovation.

A cry from the crowd:

VOICE
Hot damn! Itsa Soggy Bottom Boys!

Everett and the boys, still singing, exchange bemused looks. A shrug, and they lean into the song with a will.

Everett performs an impromptu buck-and-wing, bringing the crowd to new heights of hysteria.

PAPPY
Holy-moly. These boys're a hit!

JUNIOR
But Pappy, they's inter-grated.

PAPPY

Well I guess folks don't mind they's integrated.

Stokes is also staring at the band, frowning. He murmurs to himself:

STOKES

Wait a minute . . .

Everett catches Stokes' look. The two men look at each other, aghast.

Stokes raises his voice accusingly:

. . . you's miscegenated! All you boys! Miscegenated!

Everett raises the volume of his singing. Stokes cries out:

Get me a mike-a-phone!

A mike is thrust into his hand and he bellows into it, overwhelming the music, which the boys eventually abandon. Stokes continues bellowing into the silence:

These boys is not white! These boys is not white! Hell, they ain't even ol'-timey! I happen to know, ladies'n gentlemen, this band a miscreants here, this very evening, they interfered with a lynch mob inna performance of its duties!

The crowd stares at him, stone-faced. Stokes plows on:

It's true! I b'long to a certain secret society, I don't believe I gotta mention its name, heh-heh . . .

Nobody joins in the laugh; Stokes slowly strangles on it.

. . . Ahem. And these boys here trampled all over our venerated observances an' rich'ls! Now this-here music is *over*! I aim to –

Boos start up among the crowd.

I aim to hand these boys over to – listen to me, folks!

The boos are growing in volume. There are cries of 'More music!' and even one 'Shut up, pencil-neck!'

Listen to me! These boys desecrated a fiery cross!

More boos. Waldrip approaches and nudges the microphone away to murmur confidentially into Stokes' ear. Stokes excitedly retrieves the mike and struggles to be heard:

And they convicts! Fugitives, folks, escaped off the farm!

This cuts no ice; the boos have become overwhelming.

Folks, these boys gotta be remanded the 'thorities! Criminals! And I happen to have it from the *highest* authority that that Neegra sold his soul to the devil!

He is hit by a tomato.

The boos are deafening; the Soggy Bottom Boys, sensing opportunity, launch back into the interrupted verse of 'Man of Constant Sorrow'. The boos become wild cheers.

Stokes is being pelted by foodstuffs. Shielding himself with one arm, he bellows into the mike:

Wait a minute! Wait a minute! Is you is or is you ain't my constitchency?

INT. RUSTIC CABIN

Far up some sleepy holler. An old man in overalls and his wife sit hunched before a crystal set, listening to the tinny voice. They look at each other wordlessly, look back at the crystal set.

BACK TO BANQUET HALL

Stokes is almost drowned out by the music as his midget looks apprehensively on.

STOKES

Is you is or is you ain't –

A disgruntled audience member yanks out the microphone plug; Stokes continues to mouth the inaudible words.

Pappy is considering the crowd.

PAPPY

Goddamn! Oppitunity *knocks!*

He starts clambering up onto the stage.

Two men advance through the clapping audience holding high either end of an eight-foot rail. When they reach Stokes, other audience members help load him onto the rail.

Onstage, Pappy claps along with the audience.

As they play, the band members fearfully eye Pappy, who advances on them.

Pappy joyfully shakes his fat ass in time to the music and does a little two-step. The audience roars. The band relaxes, performing with even more gusto.

Stokes is being run through the crowd on the rail, jeered at and pelted with comestibles until he bangs out the exit.

As the song rolls into its big finish the audience roars approval, and Pappy elbows in to the microphone, beaming.

That's fine, that's fine! . . .

He drops one arm around Everett, the other around Delmar.

. . . Ladies'n gentlemens here and listenin' at home, the great
state of Mississippi (Pappy O'Daniel, Gov'nor) *thanks* the
Soggy Bottom Boys for that won-a-ful performance!

Cheers.

Now it looks like the only man in our great state who ain't a
music luvva, is my esteemed opponent in the upcomin',
Homer Stokes –

Boos.

Yeah, well, they ain't no accountin' f'taste. It sounded t'me
like he harbored some kind a hateful *grudge* against the Soggy
Bottom Boys on account of their rough'n rowdy past.

Boos.

Sounds like Homer Stokes is the kinda fella gonna cast the
first stone!

Boos.

Well I'm with you folks. I'm a f'give and f'get Christian. And
I say, well, if their rambunctiousness and misdemeanorin' is
behind 'em – It *is*, ain't it, boys?

Everett hesitates, not sure where this is going.

EVERETT

. . . Sure is, Governor.

PAPPY

Why then *I* say, by the par vested in me, these boys is hereby
pardoned!

Loud cheers prod Pappy to another level of inspiration:

And furthermore, in the second Pappy O'Daniel administration,
why, these boys – is gonna be my brain trust!

Raucous cheers.

The band beams, but Delmar leans in to Everett, worried:

DELMAR

What sat mean exactly, Everett?

EVERETT

Well, you'n me'n Pete'n Tommy are gonna be the power behind the throne so to speak.

DELMAR

Oh, okay.

PAPPY

So now, without further ado, and by way of endorsin' my candidacy, the Soggy Bottom Boys is gonna lead us all in a chorus of 'You Are My Sunshine' – ain't ya, boys?

He gives Everett a meaningful look, which Everett holds for a considering beat.

EVERETT

. . . Governor – that's one of our favorites!

Pappy returns a considered appraisal:

PAPPY

Son, you gonna go far.

The song begins.

LATER

The steps of the meeting hall. People stream out of the concert into the warm summer night.

Everett, now relieved of his beard, is walking down the steps with Penny.

EVERETT

I guess Vernon T. Waldrip is gonna be goin' on relief. Maybe I'll be able to throw a little patronage his way, get the man a job diggin' ditches or rounding up stray dogs.

DELMAR

Is the marriage off then, Miz Wharvey?

McGill. No, the marriage'll take place as planned.

EVERETT

Just a little change of cast. Me and the little lady are gonna
pick up the pieces'n retie the knot, mixaphorically speakin'.
You boys're invited, of course. Hell, you're best men! Already
got the rings.

*He raises Penny's left hand with his own to display their wedding bands
– but Penny's finger is bare.*

Where's your ring, honey?

PENNY

I ain't worn it since our divorce came through. It must still be
in the rolltop in the old cabin. Never thought I'd need it;
Vernon bought one encrusted with jewels.

EVERETT

Hell, now's the time to buy it off him cheap.

PENNY

We ain't gettin' married with *his* ring! You said you'd
changed!

EVERETT

Aw, honey, our ring is just a old pewter thing –

PENNY

Ain't gona be no weddin'.

EVERETT

It's just a symbol, honey –

PENNY

No weddin'.

DELMAR

We'll go fetch it with ya, Everett.

EVERETT

Honey, it's just – Shutup, Delmar – it's just –

PENNY

I have spoken my piece and counted to three.

She walks off.

EVERETT

Oh god*damnit*! She counted to three! Sonofabitch! You know how far that cabin is?!

His attention, and everyone else's, is drawn by a procession on the street below. A crowd carrying torches jogs behind a man in clanking leg irons and wrist manacles who is being escorted by four policemen trotting alongside, their nightsticks held across their chests in riot-ready formation.

Everett and the rest of the Soggy Bottom Boys descend the last couple of steps to meet the oncoming criminal. Delmar cries out:

DELMAR

George!

It is indeed George Nelson, grinning and game despite his heavy restraints.

GEORGE

'Lo, boys! Well, these little men finally caught up with the criminal a the century! Looks like the chair for George Nelson. Yup! Gonna electrify me! I'm gonna go off like a Roman candle! Twenty thousand volts chasin' the rabbit through yours truly! Gonna shoot sparks out the top of my head and lightning from my fingertips!

As he passes he turns to call back over his shoulder:

Yessir! Gonna suck all the power right outa the state! Goddamn, boys, I'm on top of the world! I'M GEORGE NELSON AND I'M FEELIN' TEN FEET TALL!

Delmar, smiling, shakes his head as he watches him go.

DELMAR

Looks like George is right back on top again.

BLACK

In the black we hear snuffling, growing louder, closer, slobberier.

A crack of light. We are inside a cupboard. Its door is being nosed open by an eagerly sniffing snout.

As the door swings wide the inside of the cupboard is washed with light. It contains, next to a tangled bunch of hairnets, several neatly stacked tins of Dapper Dan pomade.

PINEY WOODS

Everett, Pete, Delmar and Tommy are walking through the woods.

> EVERETT
> Well, at least you boys'll get to see the old manse – the home where I spent so many happy days in the bosom of my family – a refugium, if you will – with a mighty oak tree out front and a happy little tire swing . . .

They emerge into a clearing. The cabin stands before them. It is indeed a peaceful-looking haven with a mighty oak tree in front. There is, however, no tire swing; instead, three nooses hang from one stout limb.

> DELMAR
> Where's the happy little tire swing?

Two shotgun-wielding goons fall in behind the four men and push them forward.

Moving forward reveals, next to the oak tree, three fresh-dug graves. Standing at the far lip of each grave is a rough pine coffin.

The sheriff with mirrored sunglasses, Cooley, steps off the porch, the drooling hound at his heels.

> COOLEY
> End of the road, boys. It's had its twists and turns –

> EVERETT
> Waitaminute –

> COOLEY
> – but now it deposits you here.

The goons are shoving them toward the tree. Three gravediggers, having just finished their work, emerge from the three graves. They are shirtless black men with bandanas round their necks.

EVERETT

Waitaminute –

COOLEY

You have eluded fate – and eluded me – for the last time. Tie their hands, boys.

EVERETT

You can't do this –

COOLEY

Didn't know you'd be bringin' a friend. Well, he'll have to wait his turn –

EVERETT

Hang on there –

COOLEY

– and share one of your graves.

EVERETT

You can't do this – we just been pardoned! By the Governor himself!

DELMAR

It went out over the radio!

COOLEY

Is that right?

The leering goons, who have been lashing the men's wrists behind their backs, pause, their sadism stymied. They look to Cooley for guidance.

So too does the drooling hound.

Silence.

Finally:

. . . Too bad we don't have a radio.

The goons recover their leering grins and resume their happy task.

The gravediggers stand next to the graves, leaning on their shovels. They begin to sing a slow and dirgelike 'You've Got to Walk That Lonesome Valley'. Sweat glistens on them and trickles down their faces like tears.

PETE

God have mercy!

TOMMY

It ain't fittin'!

EVERETT

It ain't the law!

COOLEY

The law. Well the law is a human institution.

Cooley gives the faintest smile.

Perhaps you should take a moment for your prayers.

PETE

Oh my God! Everett!

DELMAR

I'm sorry we got you into this, Tommy.

PETE

Good lord, what do we do?

Pete is in tears. Tommy is terrified. Delmar bows his head to silently pray.

Everett bows his head as well. He murmurs:

EVERETT

Oh Lord, please look down and recognize us poor sinners . . . please Lord . . .

The singing of the gravediggers begins a mournful swell.

. . . I just want to see my daughters again. Oh Lord, I've been separated from my family for so long . . .

The mournfully building song is now supported by a bass more palpable than audible – the song, it seems, rising out of the earth itself.

. . . I know I've been guilty of pride and sharp dealing. I'm sorry that I turned my back on you, Lord. Please forgive me, and help us, Lord, and I swear I'll mend my ways . . . For the sake of my family . . . For Tommy's sake, and Delmar's, and Pete's . . .

The rumble is building.

. . . Let me see my daughters again. Please, Lord, help us . . . Please help us . . .

The rumble erupts into a deafening roar.

A wall of water is crashing through the hollow.

It engulfs everything and everybody. The cabin itself is ripped away; the Soggy Bottom Boys are knocked off their feet and all is noise and confusion.

UNDERWATER

A silent world. Everett tumbles in the current in natural slow motion.

Suspended around him are scores of tins of Dapper Dan pomade.

Other objects spin slowly by: framed sepia-tinted family portraits, tree limbs, a fishing pole, an outhouse door, a frying pan, a noose, an old banjo, the wild-eyed frantically paddling bloodhound, a tire with a rope tied around it.

FURTHER DOWNHILL

The churning torrent opens into a lowland to become a newly created river, fast-moving but no longer violent.

After a beat of hold on the rippling waters, the surface is broken by the up-bob of a pine coffin.

The coffin floats downstream for a beat and then Everett pops out of the water next to it, gasping for air, shaking his head clear of water, and moving his shoulders to finish freeing himself from the rope round his wrists.

Pete and Delmar emerge nearby, gasping for air.

The men hang onto the coffin, which bears them downstream. Dazed, they look around.

The inundated valley shows only the occasional roof- or treetop poking out of the newly formed river. All is quiet except for the gurgle of water.

> DELMAR

A miracle! It was a miracle!

> EVERETT

Aw, don't be ignorant, Delmar. I told you they was gonna flood this valley.

> DELMAR

That ain't it!

> PETE

We prayed to God and he pitied us!

> EVERETT

It just never fails; once again you two hayseeds are showin' how much you want for innalect. There's a perfectly scientific explanation for what just happened –

> PETE

That ain't the tune you were singin' back there at the gallows!

> EVERETT

Well any human being will cast about in a moment of stress. No, the fact is, they're flooding this valley so they can hydro-electric up the whole durned state . . .

Everett waxes smug:

> Yessir, the South is gonna change. Everything's gonna be put on electricity and run on a payin' basis. Out with the old spiritual mumbo-jumbo, the superstitions and the backward ways. We're gonna see a brave new world where they run everyone a wire and hook us all up to a grid. Yessir, a veritable age of reason – like the one they had in France – and not a moment too soon . . .

His voice trails off as he notices something:

A cottonhouse in the middle of the river is submerged to its eaves. A cow has taken refuge on its roof. It stands staring at Everett, who returns the stare.

He shakes off the vision and clears his throat.

Not a moment too soon. Say, there's Tommy!

Tommy has indeed just surfaced downstream, clinging to a half-submerged piece of furniture.

What you ridin' there, Tommy?

The furniture beneath him begins to rotate in the current and, to keep his head above water, Tommy climbs in place like a hamster on a wheel. As the chest exposes its ribbed upper half:

TOMMY

Rolltop desk . . .

STREET

Everett and Penny walk arm in arm, the seven Wharvey gals behind. The girls sing 'Angel Band' as the grown-ups talk.

EVERETT

All's well that ends well, as the poet says.

PENNY

That's right, honey.

EVERETT

But I don't mind telling you, I'm awful pleased my adventuring days is at an end . . .

He fumbles in his pocket.

. . . Time for this old boy to enjoy some repose.

PENNY

That's good, honey.

EVERETT

And you were right about that ring. Any other weddin' band would not do. But this-here was foreordained, honey; fate was a-smilin' on me, and ya have to have confidence –

He is slipping it onto her hand.

PENNY

That's not my ring.

EVERETT

– in the gods – Huh?

PENNY

That's not my ring.

EVERETT

Not your . . .

PENNY

That's one of Aunt Hurlene's.

EVERETT

You said it was in the rolltop desk!

PENNY

I said I *thought* it was in the rolltop desk.

EVERETT

You said –

PENNY

Or, it might a been under the mattress.

EVERETT

You –

PENNY

Or in my chiffonier. I don't know.

Everett shakes his head.

EVERETT

Well, I'm sorry honey –

PENNY

Well, we need that ring.

EVERETT

Well now honey, that ring is at the bottom of a pretty durned
big lake.

                    PENNY
Uh-huh.

                    EVERETT
A 9,000-hectare lake, honey.

                    PENNY
I don't care if it's *ninety* thousand.

                    EVERETT
Yes, but honey –

                    PENNY
That lake wasn't *my* doing . . .

Indignation quickens her pace. Everett keeps up, and the two are pulling forward out of frame.

                    EVERETT
Course not, honey, but . . .

We are now on the Wharvey gals who follow in a ragged bunch, still singing. From somewhere distant, through the song, we can just hear a rhythmic clack of metal on metal.

The second-to-last girl is the oldest; she holds a piece of string along which we travel, still listening to Penny and Everett, off:

                    PENNY
I counted to three, honey.

                    EVERETT
Well sure, honey, but . . .

We reach the end of the piece of string; it is wrapped around the waist of the toddler, who lingers in frame. She gazes down a quiet street at the edge of town that ends in an open field.

    . . . finding one little ring in the middle of all that water . . .

His voice, and that of the singing girls, recedes.

    . . . that is one hell of a heroic task . . .

The string is given a tug and the little girl waddles out of frame.

A train track is thus revealed in the distance. The rhythmic clack is from the hand-pumped flatcar.

The blind seer pumps the car along the distant track, singing harmony under the Wharvey gals' receding voices.

THE END

CREDITS